THE VERLINDEN WAY

by François Verlinden

scale models and dioramas

1.	Beast in the yard	3
2.	The ´Tiger` tamed	8
3.	German Marauders´ Caterer	11
4.	Double trouble	14
5.	Omar ´s back	17
6.	Dr. Todts´ orders	22
7.	Palestinian Landrover Obituary	25
8.	Dashin´ thru!	30
9.	Of no avail	34
10.	About figure painting	37
11.	Funky town	49
12.	Spectres´ castle	52
13.	Phantom servants	55

VERLINDEN PUBLICATIONS

All scale models and photography by François Verlinden unless otherwise indicated.

Text: Hans Wilms
Artwork and lay-out: Willy Peeters

ISBN 90-70932-05-9

Beast in the yard

The Panther G, subject of this diorama together with the new MDA-kit 'Ruined barn' (MDA 35011), was a simplified version of the earlier Panthers. The original hull was too complicated to produce, involving too much cutting, welding and too many jigs. Moreover, there were too many different gages of rolled armorplating. The bend in the sponson bottom was straightened, the angle of the sponson sides increased from 50° to 61° and the thickness of the plate increased. The driver's and radio-operator's hatches changed in shape. To keep shots from deflecting into the hull roof, caused by the rounded underside of the gun mantlet, the latter was changed in shape. Later Panther G types were equipped with the steel roadwheels with internal rubber spring action to save rubber, used in great quantities for the old type rubber-lined roadwheels. Eventually, the complicated procedure of interlocking the various plates was changed to simple buttwelding.

The best Panther-kit is without doubt the one from Nichimo. The basic detail is quite sufficient, although especially the hull needs some conversions to make a real G-type Panther. These changes are all illustrated on the following pages. These basically concern the driver's and radio-operator's hatch covers and cooling grids. Besides that, the typical late-war Zimmerit anti-magnetic mine paste should be simulated.

The new MDA kit represents a barn that is quite typical for the French and Belgian country side. There is an abundance of farm accessories on offer from the French company Historex to make a very interesting scene. The basic kit of the farm is already very interesting, however, there are enough possibilities for the enthousiastic detailer to make the most out of it. The fairly new set with photo-etched iron works were specially designed for this kit. Other new VP-items featured on this diorama are the embossed cardboard cobble-stones and the popular but up till now hard-to-get static grass.

The only real changes involved with the Nichimo kit are the updated cooling intake and outlet covers of the late type Panther G. All you need for the changes is some plastic sheet and a piece of mosquito netting or lace curtain.

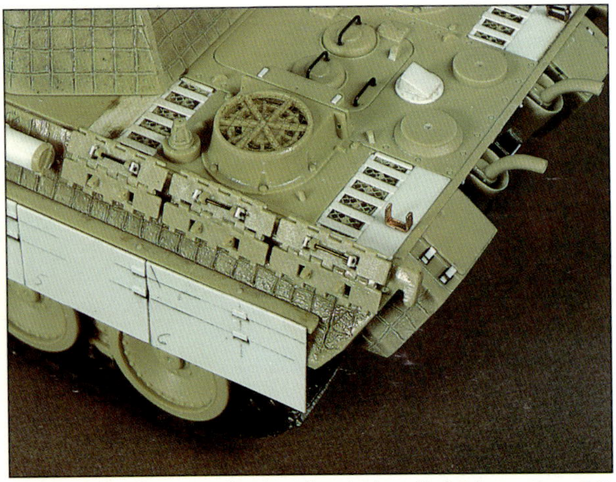

Most of the work involved in finishing the kit is consumed by super-detailing. Most kits either lack small detail or the detail is too heavy, the Nichimo Panther is no exeption to that. Many mounting points and handgrips are missing, while the trackskirts and gun cleaning-rod container are liable for improvements.

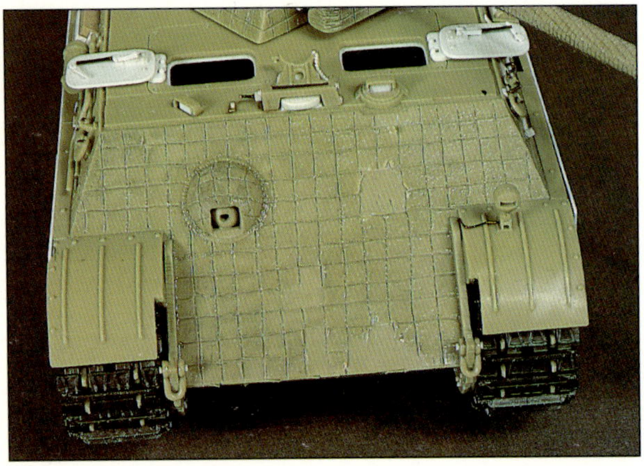

Detail of the finished, unpainted Zimmerit. To obtain the eroded areas you may either work around these spots or mask them with tape.

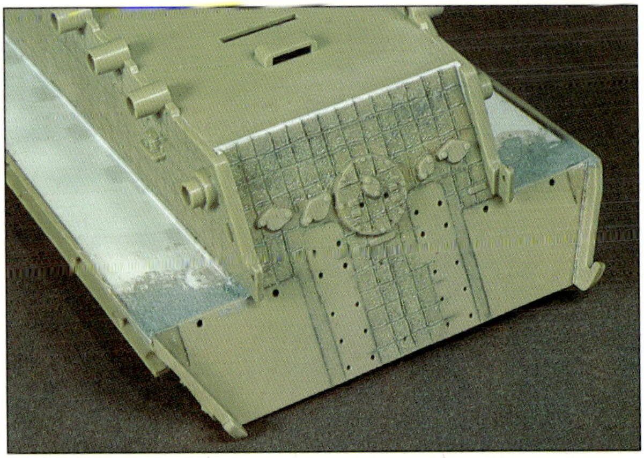

The Zimmerit pattern is drawn on the bare plastic with a pencil. Next, a liberal amount of liquid glue is applied on the surface to soften the plastic. This softened plastic is worked with a brush to obtain a rough surface. Then, the pattern lines are scribed with a knife or needle. These are then finished and you have your Zimmerit. Note that the areas where additional kitparts should go should be left smooth.

The driver's and radio-operator's hatch covers are best made anew since the kitparts are quite insufficiently detailed. Also note the detail on the barrel travel-lock, the episcopes and gun mantlet.

The finished engine deck in detail. Note the additional details from plastic sheet, rod and lace curtain.

Only the final painting and weathering brings out the best in a super-detailed kit. In case of a German tank with Zimmerit, weathering is ever so important. It should enhance the effect of Zimmerit without overdoing it.

Nicely painted figurines with a natural expression and pose are always an asset to every model. Note the very detailed, authentic throat-microphone and headset. The beautifully sculpted figures are available in the VP-program.

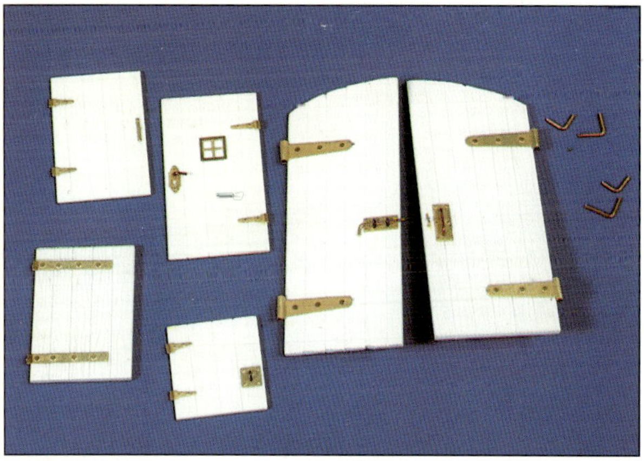

The VP Iron Works (ACDA 35006) are glued to home-made doors and shutters. The latter were manufactured from plastic sheet. The seperate planks and wood-grain pattern can easily be scribed with a needle. Doors and such could be made from real wood, but this calls for a lot of care and is quite time-consuming.

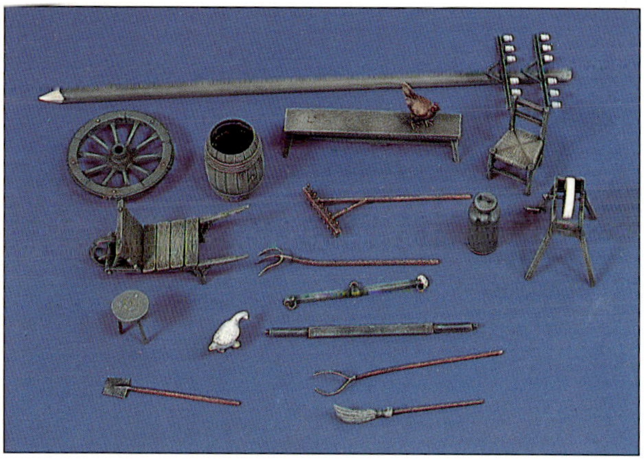

The complete selection of farm accessories. Most of the stuff was taken from the Historex-program, while some other items come from Tamiya and Italeri. Care should be taken that even these small details are finished just as superbly as the main items.

Bottom: The inside of the ruined barn was detailed as well. True, not as extensively as the erxterior, but still... If you wish, you may carry it a lot further by including stairs, interior stables, a water pump, a hay-loft, and whatever other goodies you may find in a barn.
Right: The typical farm tools and some poultry that survived the fighting that destroyed part of the barn. Just try to figure out all the details, before you know it will be an hour later.

The´Tiger`tamed

For those who feel they have seen this Tiger somewhere before, you are right! It was used to illustrate the application of battle-damage and Zimmerit in 'On target' n° 1. You are looking at the final production type Tiger, as is witnessed by the absence of a pistolport in the turret and the Panther type commander's copula. However, the tank still has the rubber-lined roadwheels. Those amongst you who have read the 'On target' book know, that this is quite a conversion. The basis is the Tamiya-kit of the very early type Tiger, with various parts of the Nichimo Tiger kit.

The tank is finished in the late war camouflage pattern of a basecoat of sand-yellow and an over-spray of green and brown. The weathering is a little special because of the traces of fire in the left sponson fueltank. You may know that iron and steel rust almost immediately after being heated up by a fire. Therefore, the area where the fire raged should be weathered in a light-brown color. It is best to use powdered pastel chalks to do so. The rest of the finishing job is pretty much standard.

Besides the Tiger, the diorama features the MDA-kit 'Ruined Rathaus', the Italeri BMW with sidecar, and two figurines from the very useful Tamiya-set 'German soldiers at rest'. Extensive use has been made of virtually all VP-acessories.

We have said it a couple of times before, you can never use enough debris on a diorama that includes a ruin. Most of the big chunks come with the kits, the small debris is on offer in sepe-rate bags.

The diorama lay-out is well-balanced as the basic rules have been followed. The higher objects are in the rear, the lower in front, and the general line is diagonal to the sides of the baseplate. All 'empty' spots have been filled, whether it be with a roadblock or a pile of rubble.

The Italeri BMW with sidecar is a beautiful model in itself. It lends itself very well to be displayed as a solitary model on a vignette or as a secondary model on a larger diorama.

Close-up of the battle-damage for those who do not have the 'On target' book. The hole in the sponson side has been made with the pyrograph. Once you have pierced the plastic you should jerk the tip around to obtain the typical rough edges. The traces of the bounced shot can also be made with the pyrograph.

Overall top-view of the knocked-out Tiger. The traces of fire are very obvious. Noteworthy is the battle damage other than the AT-grenade penetration holes, like the loose grids on the cooling air intakes, etc.

The amount of work that has to be done is obvious from this picture of the finished, yet unpainted turret. The original commander's copula was replaced by one from a Panther, a new turret ventilator has been added, as well as a cover for the loader's periscope and a projector for small mortar mines aft of the loader's hatch. The small strips on the side of the turret served to mount track-links for additional protection.

An attractive picture of the rear of the Tiger with a reproduction of a wartime picture as background.

German Marauders' Caterer

The GMC models of both Italeri and Heller are very rewarding kits. They come in three basic versions: two of Italeri, being the open cabin cargo truck and the closed cabin watertank truck, and one from Heller, the open cabin cargo truck, but this time with a fully detailed engine and a tarp.

The GMC, workhorse of the US Army in WWII, and still going strong in many armies today, is very well documented. There are numerous different versions, in fact, you may go on building just GMC's for the rest of your life. There are the cargo trucks, dump trucks, refueling trucks, workshop trucks, wreckers, radio trucks, etc.

In this case the conversion was so simple, that it is hardly worth mentioning. The open cabin of the cargo truck was replaced by the closed cabin of the watertank truck, while the tarp was taken from the Heller-kit. Further items are the 105mm Howitzer from Italeri and the Schwimmwagen and some Flak Crew figurines from Tamiya.

The scene is pretty simple. The GMC was abandonned by its crew in the panic that followed the German attacks at the start of the Ardennes Offensive. While one German takes his time to pick some of the best from an American C-ration, the other is very concerned about a possible Allied air-raid.

Nothing beats the realistic effect of the VP dry transfer vehicle markings. They can be weathered without any difficulty, while wet decals have a nasty carrier film that would show up, and it is very easy to simulate chipped letters.

The Schwimmwagen crew in detail. The officer was taken straight from the Tamiya Flak Crew. The sitting soldier was slightly converted with parts from the scrapbox. The C-ration cartons need no further comment, just look in the VP catalog. The rest of the cargo on the GMC was of course taken from various accessory-sets and the scrapbox.

Before the Schwimmwagen and figures were added, the whole was sprinkled with farina from a saltsprinkler. You should add some grains of rice or the farina will curdle. The farina should be fixed to the items with a light overspray of hairlac.

A shot of the action on the diorama. The background poster may by now be rather familiar to those who have the other Verlinden publications. Just a few posters like this take you a long way.

Both the 105mm Howitzer and Schwimmwagen are pretty accurate straight from the box and just call for a good paint and weather job.

Double trouble

The German firm J. Peddinghaus has released a 1/35 scale resin model of the WWII German navy 'Neger', a manned torpedo. The kit comes with some figures to form a diorama. Two miniature submarines, the 'Biber' and 'Seehund' are also available.

The 'Neger' (Negro) basically was a type G7E torpedo mounted under a specially adapted torpedo of the same type. The top torpedo had its warhead replaced by a crew compartment with controls to steer the craft and launch the life torpedo. The single 'captain' sat out in the open behind a plexiglass screen on the first types, but unless the sea was as smooth as a pond before a storm, the compartment was flooded by the wash. The operational types were equipped with a plexiglass dome, which posed another problem: keeping the captain alive. The normal oxygen equipment was too heavy and would further reduce the already very limited range. The solution was found in a supply of air purifying tablets as used in submarines. A great disadvantage of the dome:..... it could only be removed from the outside. The thing was a real deathtrap.

The craft was very unstable at speeds in excess of 3 knots. Moreover, at higher speeds the life torpedo could, once launched, foul the carrier and drag the thing at a speed of 30 knots towards the target. The very limited radius due to the electric propulsion (some 32 miles) meant that the operational base had to be extremely close to the target, a very impractical circumstance. A round trip meant that the craft was at sea for approximately eleven hours, with all problems of oxygen supply, navigation and avoiding detection.

The Neger was only used at Anzio and Nettuno and at Sword-beach in Normandy. After these operations the surprise element was gone, so every Ally was on the look-out. The fact that the Neger could not submerge, the plexiglass dome remained surfaced, made it a sitting duck for allied fighter pilots. An estimated 200 were destroyed, many of them by bombs and bullets from Mustangs and Thunderbolts. A further development, the 'Marder', was equipped with diving cells, but never used operationally.

To 'submerge' the carrier torpedo, there is no sense in using the life torpedo as well, you could either turn in into a waterline or place it in a cut-out in the basic material. In this case I used designer's cardboard with styrofoam in between the two layers. The various shades of green that simulate the water should be airbrushed before the torpedo is fixed in the cut-out. The gaps around the torpedo are then filled with white glue. This takes a while to do because the glue shrinks. The advantage of white glue is that it turns transparent when drying.

The mecanic that comes with the kit. The arms were replaced by some from the scrapbox to suit the desired pose. The raft was made from three halves of Tamiya oil-drums and some plastic sheet simulating planking.

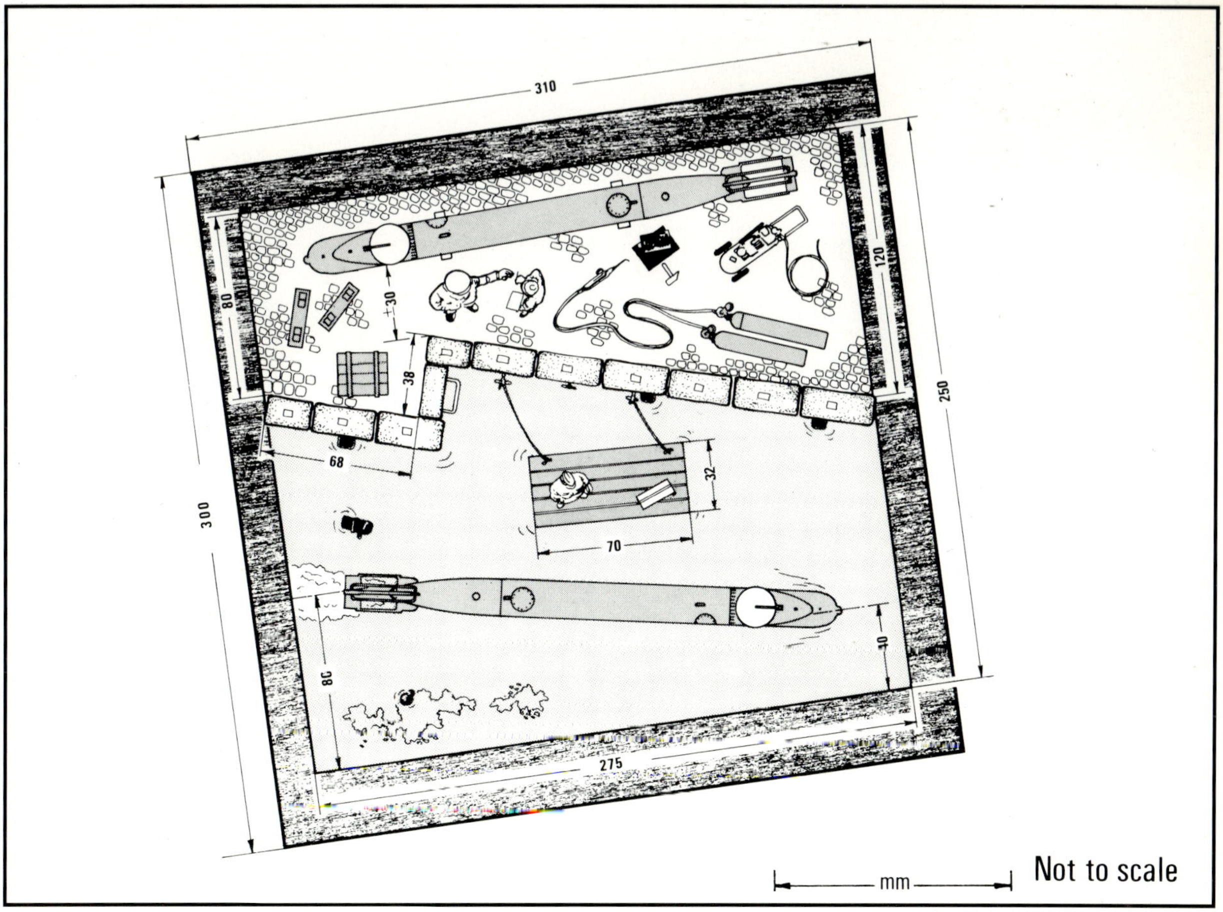

The MDA Wharf Elements were specially designed for the 'Neger'-kit. There are three basic parts that can be detailed and combined in any way you prefer. It should be noted that the buffer-poles, iron stairs and mooring rings are not included in the kit. To add some life to the scene, a second 'Neger'-kit was used and some additional German sailors were obtained from J.Peddinghaus.

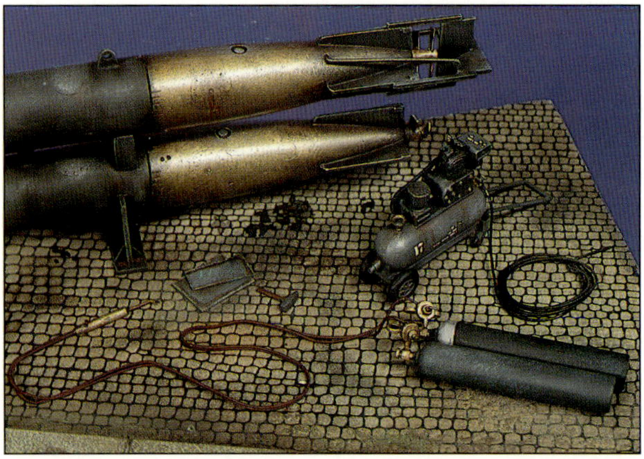

A few of those things that make a lively scene out of a simple diorama. A compressor and welding unit were taken from the Italeri 'Field Tool Shop', as well as some smaller tools. They are a must on every diorama featuring technical items.

Omar ´s back

During the past two years or so, several manufacturers have finally paid attention to modern fighting vehicles. We do not have to enumerate all the kits that have meanwhile been released.

Subject of this diorama is the latest Tamiya kit, the M2/M3 Bradley. The kit is beautiful, but let's say it straight away, not totally free of some minor mistakes. There are some distinctive differences between the M2 IFV and the M3 CFV. The IFV has ball-shaped rifle mounts on both sides and in the rear ramp with sighting episcopes directly above them. On the CFV these ball mounts and episcopes have been omitted and their respective holes blanked off with sheet stock. The Tamiya kit is wrong in the sense that, where it is supposed to be an M3 CFV, yet it does have the episcopes and ball mounts, but the latter are not complete. Therefore, the model is a mixture of the M2 and M3. The easiest way to go at it is to add the missing details on the ball mounts and thus make the M2. In order to make the M3 you would have to remove both the mounts and episcopes.

The M2/M3 was developed in order to give the infantry a capable fighting vehicle that can keep pace with the very agile M1 Abrams. Furthermore, a real infantry fighting vehicle was long overdue. The M113 was okay, as long as it was used as a bus to transport infantry to and from the frontline. However, its lack of fire power and relatively thin armor made it a sitting duck on the frontlines. The M2 is better armored, a lot faster and packs quite a punch in one single vehicle. It is equipped with the Hughes 25mm Chain Gun, a cannon that fires depleted uranium shells, powerfull enough to blast anything but a full-grown tank to pieces. To take care of tanks, it has a double TOW launcher with sufficient reloads, while a co-axial machine-gun and rifles in the six ball mounts will take care of anything on two feet that gets too close with bad intentions. Badly enough, the vehicle is so expensive, that only the heavy US divisions get their share. The lighter units and reserves will have to go on using updated versions of the old M113 as a hack.

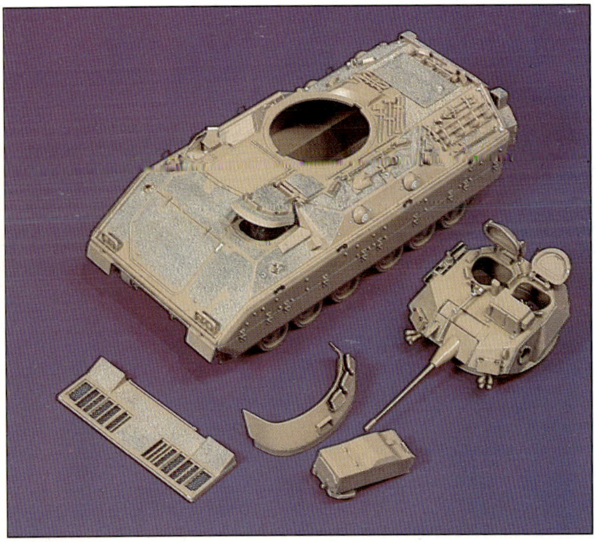

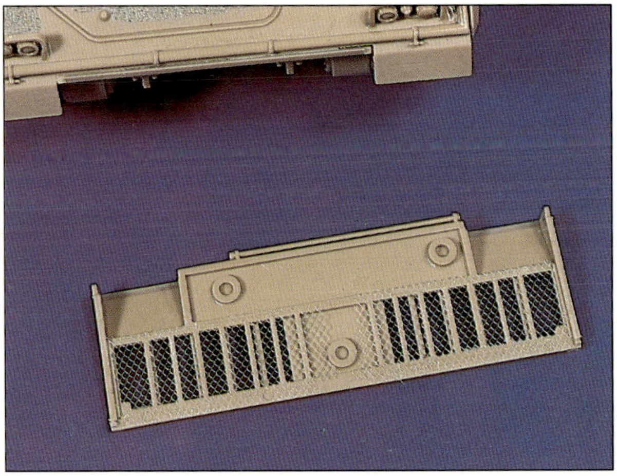

The basic kit does not leave you heartsick. As said, just the ball mounts need some extra detail, while the bow trim plate could do with a little attention as well. The rest is an enjoyable piece of cake.

A very prominent feature that really should be added, is the anti-slip coating on practically all upper surfaces. This not only keeps people from sliding off the vehicle, but also adds to the matt finish against aerial recognition.

The anti-slip coating is best simulated with fine grain sand, that should be sprinkled on a fair amount of glue that in its turn has been applied to the basic plastic. Note the areas where the anti-slip should go.

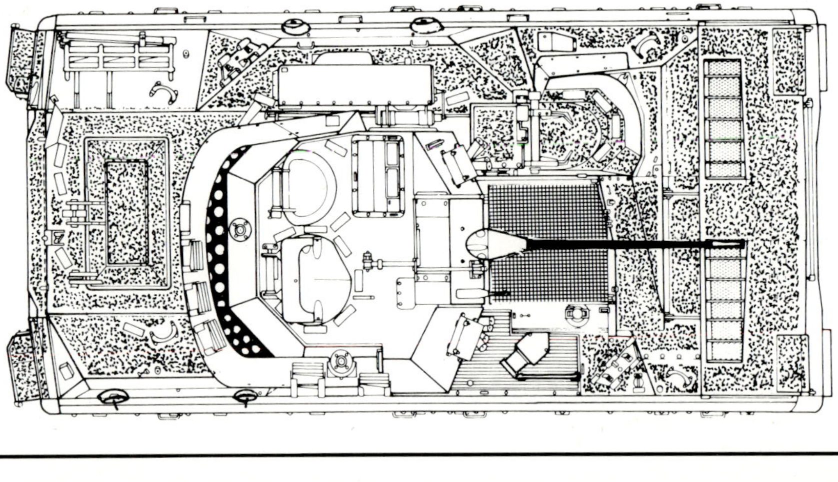

Not to scale

Once painted and weathered, the Bradley with anti-slip coating looks very impressive. The effect of the fine grain sand is very convincing, and since it is easy to apply, it is the fastest way to go.

The Tamiya M151 Ford Mutt is a model that can be used on almost every diorama involving US Army and Israeli army material. Here it has been built as a light reconnaissance vehicle, as is obvious from the MG mount.

The soldiers in the Jeep, as this vehicle is still called, are slightly converted Tamiya figures, wich are of relatively good quality. The M151 is packed with the usual personal gear, some ammo and MRE rations.

The finish obtained through attentive painting and weathering could trick anyone into believing that one is looking at a real Bradley and Ford Mutt. When you take a picture of a diorama with the correct lighting and a suitable background poster, you end up with an almost life-like photo.

The rear end of the Bradley has been liberally dusted with pastel chalks to simulate dust that was thrown up by the tracks.

A little puddle always lends a nice effect to a diorama and just about every military excersise range has a couple. They are rather easy to simulate with various shades of green paint, which by the way must be airbrushed, and a final heavy coat of gloss varnish.

Another interesting and very impressive shot of the Bradley. It illustrates to advantage the tremendous punch it packs. Of special note are the very natural looking camouflage nets. They are simple to make with VP nets, which are soaked in diluted white glue. They should then be rolled and left to dry almost completely. When they are almost dry, they should be placed on the vehicle and bent to conform to the shape of the latter.

The Bradley crew was converted by cutting the VP US tank crew 1980's apart and exchanging heads and arms. The seperately available sets with heads enable you to go even further. They feature bare heads, heads with Vietnam style jungle hats, fieldcaps, helmets old and new style, and so on.

This picture taken from above offers a good view on the gear on the hood of the Jeep. This flat surface is often used as a table top, be it to eat or to check out a staff map. The sign on the radiator grill is mandatory in Germany, just like the rotary light. Also noteworthy is the life-like appearance of the soil.

Dr. Todts´orders

The renowned Pillbox, the nickname denotes the small size and shape, is one of the simplest forms of enclosed concrete fortifications. Often it did not more have than one room, could not hold more than one MG-squad or observation party, sometimes did not even have a steel entrance door. The bunker was mostly used for perimeter defence or as a forward observation post. You could find them in the forward lines of fortification sites as a pinpoint-defence for large naval gun bunkers or as observation bunker for trenched artillery.

When used to defend large naval gun sites, they acted in addidition to the gun bunker's own defence system. Anyone who knows a thing or two about bunkers, is familiar with the machine-gun ports that can be found next to the entrance(s).

Since the Pillbox acted as some sort of surprise package in the very front-line, they were heavily camouflaged. They were dug in as far as possible, the remainders were covered up with camouflage nets and vegetation. Of course, the porthole, ventholes and entrance had to be left uncovered.

The MDA-kit is simple in the way that it comes in just a few easy-to-assemble parts. The sloping wall next to the porthole is to fysically limit the arc of fire of the MG in order to keep it from firing into own installations. The battle-damage can be detailed at your own discretion.

The figurines used on the diorama are both metal castings of Cheshire Volunteer. Extensive use has been made of various VP diorama accessories like barbed wire, camouflage nets, static grass and so on.

Contrary to normal procedures, the bunker was finished completely with camouflage nets, sandbags and such. Before it was incorporated into this diorama, it was intended for another project. The bunker has been fixed to the baseplate, a block of styrofoam is glued to the already finished sandbag wall protecting the entrance, and additional sandbags from epoxy-putty were added. Note that the styrofoam has been primed with an earth-brown waterbase paint.

The battle-damage to the pillbox in detail. The reinforcements have been simulated with copper wire that was inserted in pre-drilled holes. By the way, the plaster material of which the bunker consists is very easy to cut and machine. Note the bright spots, traces of recent small arms fire.

The entrance of the Pillbox tells a story of its own. Obviously the bunker was captured very recently. The German weapons are still lying around, while the souvenir-hungry allied soldiers usually took anything that still was in good working order. The machine-guns, mines, handgrenades and ammo boxes were tak
from the Tamiya-set 'German infantry weapons'. The pile of empty cartridges are lengths of sprue r
brass.

A close-up of the Cheshire figurines. The American MP and British sergeant are obviously discussing further procedures after the capture of a German defence line. MP's just behind the front-line were mostly involved in traffic control and care for prisoners of war.

A closer look at the quite heavily defended entrance shows quite an array of abandoned weapons, a real treat for many combat soldiers. Noteworthy are the loaded 'Panzerfäuste', the German equivalent of the British PIAT.

Pillboxes could be found virtually anywhere. Going by the vegetation, this may very well be a heath, so it could be anywhere in France, the Benelux or Germany. Succesful photography with good background material is a very challenging part of plastic modeling.

Palestinian Landrover Obituary

The conflicts in the Middle East always are a great source of inspiration for many dioramas. The Israeli armed forces as subject are very interesting, since they have used a great variety of vehicles, aircraft and weapons and actually still do. They employed about everything you can think of, including Soviet material.

This diorama features an Israeli M109A1 passing a knocked-out Landrover of the PLO, a scene familiar to anyone who has ever watched the news-reels.

The M109 is of course the Italeri kit, since there is no other. As already mentioned in 'The Verlinden Way' volume IV, this model is far from being ideal and way below today's standards. But, if you want an M109, it will have to do. Luckily enough, the Israeli M109's are all of the A1 or A3 type, which can be built almost straight from the box.

Although it may not be very obvious at first sight, the Landrover also is from Italeri. It was converted into the short wheelbase vehicle by cutting the chassis and sides. Reason for this being that there is no positive evidence the PLO ever used the long wheelbase version, but for sure used the short one. The Soviet machinegun was taken from the T-62 from Tamiya, while the mount was custom made.

The typical Lebanon scene is kept very simple at first sight, but involves quite some hidden work, that is not all together obvious when looking at it at first.

The pictures on this page show the major items of the diorama. As you can see, the M109 kit is badly in need for improvements and additional basic details. Next to that, there are many details typical for Israeli vehicles, like for instance the bars welded to the hull sides. The picture of the painted and weathered M109 speaks for itself. The construction of the PLO Landrover is very simple. The model has to be cut into pieces to make the short wheelbase version, no problem for a modeller with a little experience. Further you need to make the mount for the MG, which is easy to do with some plastic rod and sheet. As these mounts were made at random, you should not bother too much about the looks.

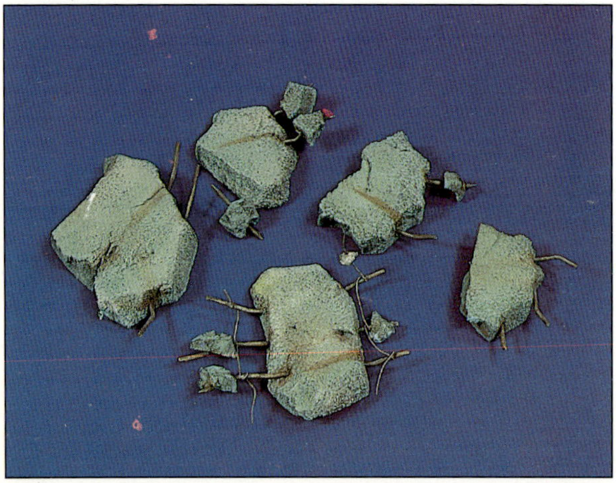

The chunks of concrete, remainders of a building, should be provided with reinforcements. This is just a matter of drilling holes and inserting pieces of copper wire or plastic rod.

The lay-out of the diorama has been established and the scene is taking shape. All that remains to be done now is to finish the groundwork and add the small accessories.

Remainders of PLO supplies next to the Landrover. The cardboard boxes were taken from the VP-set with military cardboard boxes. The ammo-crates can be found in many accessory sets, but can also be home-made quite easily. The empty shell containers were made on a lathe in this case, but you can also use short lengths of brass tubing.

The cargo floor and sponsons of the Landrover are covered with empty cases. These are simply pieces of plastic rod, painted brass. Note the bullet holes in the fender and transparencies. The hood shows traces of fire in the engine compartment.

This view reveals more interesting details like the remainders of what could have been a concertina roadblock, an old gate and a typical Israeli signpost. You should note the amount of debris close to the wall.

A close-up of the debris, barbed wire and gate. Note that all items are optically bonded together by dusting them with the same shade of powdered pastel chalks.

The usual Israeli military signposts are smart in the sense that they carry a light to make them more obvious at night for the drivers. The lamp is shielded so it does not shed any light sideways.

The VP Israeli tank crew fits the finished M109 very well. Their natural pose and realistic looks will enhance the authenticity of any model for that matter. The Landrover obviously lost a wheel while bumping over the fence along the road. Note the very realistic effect of the dirtroad.

Dashin´ thru!

Another rewarding object for the military modeler is the renowned Sherman. There are enough basic versions on offer to allow you to go for a large selection of converted models. The only version we still miss is the one with the HVS-suspension, which would be so easy to make for Italeri in particular, since they only have to change the suspension and tracks of an existing model. The old kit from Tamiya is way out of scale. Maybe someone will see the light some day.

In WWII the Sherman was subject to many changes, many of them were carried out in the field, sometimes even at platoon level. Take any one squadron of Shermans, you will not find two vehicles that are exactly alike.

Thus, the Sherman model offers a great deal of possibilities. You can change the upper hull and turret of both the Tamiya and Italeri models around, swap tracks, make a composite hull and so on.

This diorama features the Tamiya hull and suspension combined with the Italeri turret and the new MDA-kit 'Ruined Ardennes Farm'. The model has been detailed extensively, while the typical extra armor plates were added. The stock Shermans were no match for the better armed and armored German heavies and suffered a high attrition rate, mainly due to the dreaded '88'. Therefore, the first concern of experienced crews receiving new vehicles was to remove the big, bright white stars that formed such a perfect aiming mark for the German gunners. Secondly, they roamed every depot looking for armor plating to weld or bolt onto their tanks, usually at the most vulnerable areas like ammo stores, fuel tanks and glacis plate. This additional protection was just enough to survive the first hit and have a change to retreat.

This general view shows all the additional armored protection. The plates were bolted to the glacis plate and turret, with spacers in between. The first, by the way unintentional, spaced armor emerged, a type of armor that is so common in our days.

The rear of the Tamiya hull is quite satisfying. Just a touch of additional detail does the job. The spare track links have been omitted and replaced by a jerrycan and .50 cal ammo crate.

The additional armor plate on the glacis plate necessitates removal and repositioning of the lights, lifting lugs and gun barrel travel lock. I chose to use the driver's and co-driver's hatch covers of the Italeri kit, since the detail is more crisp. As with all tank models, the periscope mounts needed extra details.

The turret needs quite some additional detail, apart from the armor plates. The .50 cal travel mount is too basic, the periscope mounts need no further comment, the spent-case port must be filled around the frame, etc.

Apart from the things mentioned above, you should also note the simple back-up sight next to the gunner's periscope, the dust cover mounting strip on the turret just behind the gun mantlet and the home-made .30 cal MG mount. This simply is a piece of copper wire.

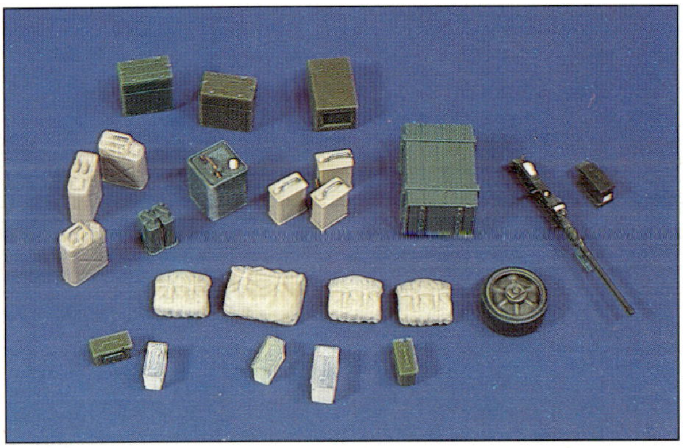

A selection of the usual stuff US tank crews carried around on their hack. These are just the military goodies. Most of the items are resin casts, available in good hobby shops.

The usual pile of equipment on US Army vehicles. American soldiers are true masters when it comes to turning their mount into something that looks more like a cargo truck than a fighting vehicle.

Part of the large debris comes with the MDA-kit. It should be painted and weathered, just like the ruin itself, before it is fixed to the diorama.

It is always wise to work in levels on your diorama. The best material to use for elevations over 1 cm. is styrofoam, since it is very light and easy to work up.

Besides the natural pose of the crew, you should also take the time to take a closer look at the equipment on the turret.

The abandoned dolly of a German '88' is a left-over from the diorama project shown on the next pages. Items like these are perfect to fill empty corners.

26

1893

Of no avail

Remember the dolly of the '88' on the previous diorama? This is where it stems from. You see that you do not have to use all kit items on one and the same diorama. They always come in handy on another one.

The scene itself again is quite simple. A US Army officer is seen inspecting one of the dreaded '88's. This one obviously still is intact. Most of the abandoned weapons had their tube blown to pieces.

What makes this diorama so attractive are the very nicely detailed MDA 'Rathaus' and the very realistic debris with accessories scattered all over. In that respect this diorama is well worth taking a closer look. As stressed before, sufficient debris is important, but it is equally important to place it well. You should not use chunks of concrete for debris close to a building where only brick has been used in construction. It is the small detail that the true diorama fanatic judges a scene by. Again the need for good documentation is apparent.

A perfect diorama, what more can be said? The effective use of simple accessories not only keeps the expenses down, but also tells a great deal about your craftsmanship.

RATHAUS
Verdunkeln!
WAFFEN
Hitlerstrass

Am Ende steht der Sieg!
WAFFEN

Hitlerstrasse

About figure painting

Many people have asked us over the years to devote a , or part of a, publication to figure-painting. Well,... here it is!

A number of people seem to have quite a lot of problems with figure-painting. This must basically be due to a severe lack of knowledge of materials, since the painting itself is not really that difficult, but merely a matter of experience. Do not think that by just reading these paragraphs, you will be able to master figure-painting right from the start. Just a few lucky ones might, but that is because they are natural-born artists. But you do not have to be an artist to be able to paint figures reasonably well. You just have to have a sound knowledge of the materials you are working with, plus a good deal of practice. For most people there is no way around these two basic rules. Some may get the hang of it a little faster than others, but if you want to master figure-painting you better be prepared to spend some time on it, or else you will have to be content with the results you have been getting up till now.

There is one more thing that needs to be said. Do not ever try to copy someone! It will not work, because the only result will be: ... a bad copy, that will not attract any positive attention from anybody! Starting with the basics, you have to develop your own style. If it should resemble someone else's style, no sweat, as long as you are painting in your own way and do not try to copy.

Let us now get to the basics. Materials for instance. For good paint jobs you need both high quality enamels and oil-paints. The enamels are used for painting clothes and accessories. All flesh parts are painted with oil-paints only! There is just one exception to that last rule: the priming of the flesh parts. Here you should use a sand yellow enamel. All the rest is nothing but oil-paint, a rule you should remember for the rest of your modeling carreer. Of course there is a reason for these rules. You will find it in the basic differences between the enamels and oil-paints. Since we are talking about matt enamels, we have already mentioned one of the differences. Enamels are matt, oil-paints are glossy. Clothes are always matt, with a few exceptions, but, you may have noticed it, human skin is always glossy, much to the dislike of most women. Secondly, enamels dry fast, oil-paints do not. Since the most complicated part of figure-painting is getting the skin parts right, you do not want fast drying paint. But it will do perfectly for clothing. The last major difference lies in the pigmentation of the paints. Oil-paint is extremely smooth, where enamels tend to have a somewhat heavier pigment, while there also is a difference in medium (bonding agent).

So, what paint do you want to buy? First the oil-paints: you would need Burnt Sienna, Raw Umber, Yellow Ocre, Cadmium Yellow, Cadmium Red and Titanium White. These colors are all you need to obtain all basic skin colors plus their variants. The enamels depend on the color of the clothing, but there is one color you always need: 8th Army Desert Yellow or Afrika Korps Desert Yellow, preferably from Humbrol. Why Humbrol? I feel that it is still the best brand of paint when you have to work with a brush. Most of the other brands give you a mediocre coverage.

It is adviseable to use the thinners recommended by the manufacturers, i.e. for Humbrol paints you need Humbrol thinner. Not that there are no compatible thinners, but when taking another than the brand's own, you run the risk of meeting unforseen problems. Why look for trouble when you can easily avoid it? To thin oil-paints you can use ordinary turpentine. When you start using the special mediums that artists do, the oil-paint either dries too fast or too slow. Turpentine works beautifully and you need it anyway to clean your brushes.

Talking about brushes, get yourself a couple good ones. Good quality lasts longer! You would need a few pointed brushes ranging from 000 to about 4 and a few flat brushes, not too wide, all preferably in pure sable.

Now that you have all your materials, we can turn to the figurines. You cannot just take them straight from the box, glue the parts together and start to paint. First you have to remove all casting seams with a knife, file, sanding paper and wire wool. This should be done very attentively since remainders of seams are very disturbing.

Then you can assemble the parts, but not before you have test-fitted them. It happens quite often that you have to correct a few things. After assembly you will have to fill possible seams. With figurines you always have a few. For plastic figures you can either use a plastic filler (Stucco from Mo-Lak is very good), or an epoxy putty. For metal figures it is epoxy putty only, unless you soft solder the parts. It is best to wipe off the excess filler or putty with a damp cloth immediately after application. It saves you a lot of sanding afterwards.

Before you start to paint, you need to remove all dirt, dust and grease from the material. This is best done with a light wash of either thinner or alcohol. In case of a metal figurine, you have to remove the oxyde. Here you need a steel brush or wire wool. Careful, lead-pewter oxyde is not very healthy! Wash your hands thoroughly before you touch food. Polish till the parts are shiny. When you have assembled and filled a metal figurine you should prime it with a metal primer, since enamels and oil-paints do not adhere to metal. Get yourself a spraycan with car primer, spray a little in a jar and apply it with a brush. Let dry thoroughly.

It is best to temporarily fix the figure to a base of some sort, for instance a small plastic box or plasticard, so you do not have to touch it while painting. It is a waste of time to have to restore damaged paint over and over again.

The first step in the actual painting concerns the skin parts. Why? Imagine you have finished the clothes to your satisfaction and louse up on the skin parts. The paint on the latter has to come off, so you have to wash it off with turpentine. Bye-bye beautiful clothing! So, paint the skin parts first. We will look at it step-by-step.

Apply a base-coat of desert yellow and let dry for at least 48 hours. This is important. When the base-coat is not thoroughly cured, you are bound to damage it, which means you have to start all over again.

What is described in the next paragraphs, is also illustrated by the color pictures hereafter. The first step is to apply a heavy coat of barely thinned mixture of equal parts of Burnt Sienna, Raw Umber and Yellow Ocre (see picture of the color chart). This is then removed with a flat brush, so there are only remainders of the mixture left in the cavities of the sculpture and just a light film on the raised parts.

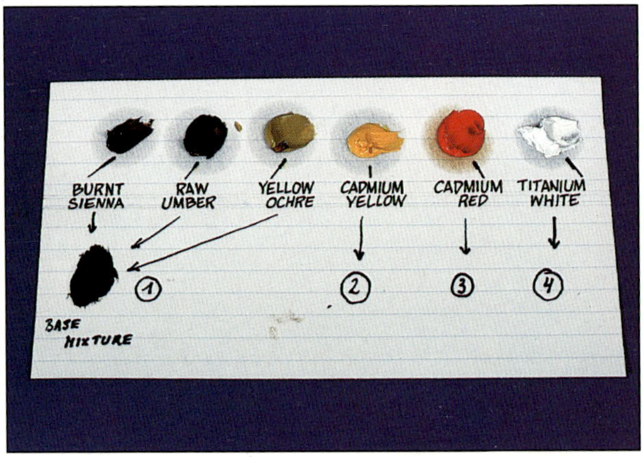

So far for the easy part. The tougher part of painting the skin, and especially the face, is getting the light and dark shades right. In other words, getting the expression on that face. This is done with the lighter colors like Yellow Ocre, Cadmium Yellow and White. In most cases you have to mix them. Apply the colors with a narrow, flat brush and blend them. You should avoid abrupt changes in shades, they should feather into each other.

There is an easy trick to find out where the dark and lights parts should go. Hold the figurine under a lamp and look at it with your eyes almost closed, so you only see through your lashes. You will immediately see the shadow areas. Basically, they go under eye-brows, nose, chin, ears, etc. In general, on all parts that face down. The lightest parts are the nose, the cheeck-bones, the forehead, top of the ears, and so on. Of course, this only applies to bare-headed figures. When they wear a hat or helmet, most of the face is in the shadow. You also have to take the complexion into account. Is the person pale or tanned, a blond caucasian or a dark-haired latino, it all matters. A pale complexion calls for extremely subtile drybrushing with a light pink (a mixture of Yellow Ocre, Red and White). This should hardly be noticeable. The lips need some attention too. Do not paint them ruby red, but rather a purple-brown shade and ... do not overdo it. The upper-lip is mostly in the shade, so it is quite dark brownish. The lower-lip catches more light, thus is a lot lighter. Moreover, lips are almost always moist, so they are shiny. This effect can be enhanced by blending a little white into the purple here and there. A stubbly beard can be simulated by carefully drybrushing the area with a mixture of black and a touch of blue.

Some people prefer to paint the white of the eyes before they start on the rest of the face. Others do it afterwards. It does not really matter, just take care that the white is not too big. The pupil takes up the larger part of the eye. Teeth, when visible, should be painted off-white, plain white is much too bright.

Painting hair is a different story. In case it is sculpted in some way, it is not too tough as when it is just one smooth surface. When you have a pyrograph, you can simulate the strands of hair with the pointed tip. Set the pyrograph at moderate heat, or you will go too deep. Any threads that remain, can be removed with wire wool. The easiest hair color to paint is black or brown. Start with a base-coat of black and drybrush with either dark or medium brown. Blond hair is a different ball-game. The base-coat is desert yellow. Drybrush with a mixture of desert yellow and white with a touch of brown here and there. You will have to go through a lot of practicing and experimenting before you obtain a satisfactory result. Every figurine seems to have its own problem in this respect. Moreover, hair can be very shiny. Take for instance raven black hair of orientals. It sometimes seems to be blueish. You will have to drybrush the black base-coat with very dark blue with a touch of white here and there to simulate the shine. When the paint is thoroughly cured, you may want to polish it with a soft cloth to enhance the shine.

Painting faces - step by step

The metal heads have been primed with light grey car primer and the skin parts received their desert yellow base-coat.

The basic mixture of Burnt Sienna, Raw Umber and Yellow Ocre has been applied.

Most of the mixture has been removed with a large, flat brush. The mixture only remains in the cavities of the sculpture.

The lighter colors are applied and blended. Note the shadow areas.

The lighter colors have been blended and a beginning has been made with painting details like the teeth.

The face is completely finished. Note the eyes and lips. Part of the uniform has been painted in the basic colors.

The uniform is completely finished. Note the shading and detail painting.

The complete collection of finished heads. It should be noted that these heads are fairly large, so do not think you can obtain this kind of detail on 1/35 scale figures.

Painting uniforms

Painting uniforms is easier than painting faces, but you should not take it too lightly either. It is basically a matter of interpretation. It is fairly easy to paint the uniform in the colors specified by the manufacturer or the author of some or another book on uniforms, whether they be 15th century or WWII. Take for instance a WWII German regular Wehrmacht uniform. It is denoted as being

Field Grey. Okay, you paint the uniform of your figurine Field Grey, add a few shadows, period. What happens, is that it comes out all wrong. The uniform may be Field Grey all right, but it does not look Field Grey. The dark areas seem to be dark green, the lightest areas seem to be lighter than Field Grey. The same goes for the US type olive green combat uniforms. The shaded areas seem to be almost black, while the light areas are a pale green. We have not yet mentioned civilian clothes, but it is needless to say that the same applies here. In this respect you should also remember never to use bright colors. Always go for the soft pastel tones. This means you have to tone down the bright colors with white or dark grey.

The verb 'seem' has been used quite a lot in the last few sentences, and it has been done on purpose. You should not use the actual denoted colors, but try to match the colors you 'seem' to be seeing. The general idea is to fool the eye. That is where interpretation comes in. This is not always easy, since you do not always have a good color picture of a particular uniform at your disposal. However, a little imagination will help you a lot. Try to get all the available pictures and, when walking in the street, start to look at people's clothes. Note the light and dark areas, the tones of different colors, the visible details at a given distance, etc. In other words, try to develop the awareness of the artist and practice it as often as you can. Try over and over again and you will find that you start to be content with the result at a certain moment. You will slowly develop a 'feeling' for the correct colors and shades.

We can help you on your way by giving the basic colors of the uniforms that are regularly seen in plastic modeling. For the US type olive green combat uniform you should use a mixture of equal parts of Humbrol US Marines Green and Humbrol Matt 29 as base-coat. A base-coat should dry thoroughly and you may seal it with a water-base varnish like Polly S. The dark areas should be shaded with the basic mixture plus some black. This mixture is best applied with a fine pointed brush and it should be diluted enough to make it flow into the cavities of the sculpture quite easily. When this is dry, you can highlight the light areas with Matt 29 with some white added. All these colors should be blended into each other with darker and lighter tones of the three basic mixtures. In general, the webbing of US soldiers is Humbrol Khaki Drill HM8. Drybrushing should be done with a lighter shade of the same basic color.

German WWII uniforms should be painted with a base-coat of Field Grey HM6. The dark areas are shaded with Khaki HF1. Highlighting is done by drybrushing with a mixture of two parts of Field Grey and one part of grass green. German webbing is basically black or brown leather. The base-coat of black should be drybrushed with very dark brown or medium brown respectively.

For British WWII uniforms you need just one basic color. The base-coat is simply Matt 29. Dark areas are shaded with Matt 29 plus some black, highlighting is done with Matt 29 plus some white. The color of the webbing is the same as with the US uniforms: Khaki Drill HM8.

Most postwar uniforms closely ressemble the US combat uniforms which are basically painted in US Marines Green HP5. Shading is effected with Khaki HF1 and highlighting is best done with light green and olive (French Artillery Green MC21). The colors to use for modern US Army camouflage uniforms are: Khaki Drill HM8 as base-coat and US Marines Green HP5, Hull Red HN5 and Matt Black 33 for the colored specks. Of course the shading and highlighting of camouflaged uniforms is quite difficult and should be done with great care in order not to obscure most of the specks.

The WWII German camouflage uniforms are very complex and consist of many colors in many patterns. Basically the colors are: sand(HP1), green(HP5) and red-brown(HN5). The general winter camouflage consists of a base-coat of neutral grey. Drybrushing is done with pure white. You may add a very light shade of Matt 29 to simulate the dirt that accumulates of the cloth.

For other uniform colors you would have to consult your documentation. There are many good books with plenty of references. Of course, the colors of civilian clothes depend on your own preference, but the same principals are applicable.

Uniform accessories like buckles, buttons, insigna and so on are painted last. Their outline is automatically shadowed when you paint the uniform. Remember never to paint metal parts in pure metal paints like silver or copper. They will be too shiny. Always mix a little grey or medium brown under the metal paint. The same that has been said about the leather belts of German uniforms is generally applicable to combat boots, whether they are black or brown.

A last tip as finishing touch. To visually tie the figurine to the diorama, you may dust a little powdered pastel chalk of appropiate color on the lower parts of the body. This will enhance the life-like appearance.

Page 42

Step 1

The metal figurine of a 'Hitlerjugend' soldier has been primed and the face painted. The field cap and coat received a base coat of dark green.

Step 2

Coat and cap are drybrushed with a lighter shade of green and field grey.

Step 3

The belt, ammo pouches and boots are primed matt black. The basic color for the Panzerfaust is dark green.

Step 4

The belt, pouches and boots are drybrushed with brown. The details like insignia, buttons and buckle are painted with toned down silver. The Panzerfaust is drybrushed with light grey and some black stencilling is added with thinned black paint.

Page 43

Step 1

A Panzergrenadier in winter camouflage dress. After the flesh parts have been finished, the camouflage clothing is painted with a base coat of medium grey, sealed with water-base matt varnish.

Step 2

A thin brown wash is applied to darken the shadow areas.

Step 3

The whole is drybrushed with matt white. Do not overdo this. Winter camouflage clothes gather dirt as well. The shoes, belt and metal parts of the rifle are painted matt black.

Step 4

The black leather belt parts are drybrushed medium grey. The rifle stock is finished with Burnt Sienna oil paint.

Simple conversions

The way figurines come, packed with seperate arms and sometimes heads and legs, allows you to go for some simple conversions. Simple but effective. Apart from changing details like belt and ammo pouches for instance, you can make any figurine you like, with a few exeptions. Changing a standing figurine into a kneeling one for instance is a different story. Here you would need appropriate legs from the scrapbox or you would have to sculpt them yourself, a procedure for the talented happy few.

The above goes for plastic figurines. Up till some time ago you had to settle for the items on offer, where metal figurines are concerned. No seperate, interchangeable heads, seperate arms that only fitted that one figurine, etc. Since VP have started to release their metal figures, this problem belongs to the past. The arms that come with a figurine, mostly fit other figurines as well as there are three sets with six different heads for use with the VP figures or other metal or plastic figurines.

There is too much to converting figurines. Changing arms only calls for some small adaptions, something you need to do with most of the original arms anyway. There is absolutely no objection against combining a metal figurine with plastic arms and vice versa. Plastic arms have the advantage that you can alter their position by carefully warming up the plastic of the elbow part and bend it. You may try to bend metal arms just a little, but succes is not guaranteed.

The VP heads will fit any 53mm or 35 or 32 scale plastic or metal figurine. The procedure of changing heads is rather simple. Using a razor saw, you cut off the original head. The VP heads come with rather long necks. Such a long neck fits a hole that you should drill in the figurine. A little test-fitting is necessary to get the position right. It is best to use cyanoacrylate to fix the metal heads to either another metal or plastic figure. When you have drilled carefully, not too much filling should be necessary. You may of course turn the heads in any direction you like. Left, right, up or down, everything is possible, although the last two possibilities require a somewhat larger hole and consecutive filling.

The pictures on this page illustrate some of the numerous possibilities offered through the VP program.

Painting camouflage uniforms

Camouflage uniforms slowly but surely take the place of the good old olive green combat dress, as has been used by virtually all western armies since WWII. The US Army has completely changed over to the so-called four-color Woodland camouflage, while other western nations have already equipped their special forces with camouflage uniforms.

This inevitably means that the modeler can not get around painting camouflage uniforms, where he immediately faces a range of problems. Because there are so many patches of different colors, you have to use darker shades of same to obtain the medium range shades. The darkest shades always come pretty close to being very dark brown or black, so there is no problem here.

However, the medium range shades serve to fade the darkest areas into the lighter parts. These shades tend to follow the color(s) of the cloth. This means you have to provide for darker shades of each camouflage color used on a particular uniform.

It is not always wise to add just a touch of black to darken a specific color, since this might change the tone all together. Sometimes you have to go for a dark complementary color of the tones you are using. It is mainly a matter of trial and error, so before tackling the shading on figurines sporting a camouflage uniform, you better start experimenting on a piece of scrap, or better yet, on one of those monsterous figures you sometimes find in AFV-kits. You do not want to use those on a diorama anyway.

The basics of painting camouflage uniforms are not any different from those that apply to the general painting of models. After cleaning the material the figurine is made of and finishing the flesh parts, you should start by applying the lightest of the camouflage colors. The reason for this is obvious, light colors do not give you as good a coverage as dark colors, so you do not want to apply them over the latter. For further

procedures it is imperative that the first coat of paint be allowed to dry thoroughly, so the bonding gets fully cured. If not, the subsequently applied paint will dissolve the bonding agent and the whole will come off. So allow for at least 12 hours curing time. The same rule apllies to the consecutive patches of paint wherever they overlap. To avoid all possible problems you may want to apply a coat of matt varnish over the first coat of paint. This not only seals the base coat for further painting, but also allows you to remove paint in case you are not satisfied with the looks of the camouflage patches.

The painting of camouflage uniforms in sequence. You should not worry too much about getting the colors exactly correct. First of all, the cloth was produced in batches, resulting in differences in colors, secondly, after some sessions in the laundry, the colors are all bleached.

A lance corporal of the English military police from Phoenix.

Some more examples

Next page

Series 77 produce a fine range of figurines from various periods and not only army personnel. The top pictures sport a beautiful WWII USAAF fighter pilot. The artwork on the back of the leather jacket is a personal choice decal on offer in the Micro Decal range.

The bottom pictures show a Series 77 figurine of a US soldier from the Vietnam era.

A Series 77 WWII GI fully geared up. Notable is the shading of the difficult to paint olive drab uniform.

OUT HOUSE
MOUSE

Funky town

A vignette can be described as a very small diorama that features one or more very small items, like in this case a figurine. There are some very good reasons to include a vignette or two to your collection of dioramas. First of all you may want to paint and display a very nice figurine without having to build a full-out diorama where the figurine disappears in the whole, nor do you want to show it of on a mere wooden base.

Secondly you attract more attention to the main object of a scene, that happens to be rather small, but still needs some sort of background to display it to advantage. This way you still have a diorama, but one that does not take up too much space.

A illustrated here, you can also get away from the usual square diorama base. Many arts & crafts shops hold a large stock of various sizes and shapes of beautifully machined wooden plates, that are normally used as lamp stands, mounts for different sorts of badges, ornaments, etc... These are perfect as display base for any small diorama you can think of. When thoroughly sanded and varnished, they can really enhance the looks of an attractive diorama.

The basic construction of a vignette is not any different from that of a large diorama, as can be seen on the next pages. The same basic rules apply as well. The lower items in front, the higher in the back, but there is no way you can get around that with those small scenes. In that respect it is a pretty good training to handle the basics of diorama construction.

There is one special aspect to pay attention to. Never pack a vignette with too much detail. Since it serves to display small items in the first place, too many accessories would distract the attention from the main object(s). When looking at any kind of diorama, it should be immediately obvious what the main object is. This is no problem with dioramas involving a vehicle or aircraft, but it gets tougher to make out a figurine amidst a pile of all sorts of accessories. In this respect, planning a vignette is in some cases more difficult than planning a large diorama.

This vignette features two figurines you have seen before, used to illustrate uniform painting. The obviously not too confident boy from the 'Hitlerjugend' in his oversize coat and the experienced Panzergrenadier are precautiously watching an air-raid, ready to run for cover should the rain of steel get too close.

Spectres' castle

Aircraft dioramas, small or large scale, have long been a problem due to the lack of sufficient accessories, what's worse, any specific accessories at all. There was hardly any ground equipment at all, just Esci had some stuff on 1/48 scale on offer, but this was limited to a tractor, towing bar, hydraulic lift, a trailer and some figures. But no power supply, generator, ground cooling, etc... And as said, just on 48th scale. There was nothing on 72nd scale, not even figures. Many would like to see equipment on 32nd scale, but this would be a commercial risk to produce, so this will remain a matter of scratchbuilding. No manufacturer will venture into producing them.

However, already some time ago, Hasegawa got the message that something new was due to keep the modeling market going. So they carefully probed the market by releasing a few kits with weapon sets. These proved to be succesful, so recently they marketed two sets with ground equipment on 72nd scale. Let us hope the same will follow on 48th scale. By the time this book was compiled they had announced a set with USAF pilot/groundcrew on 72nd scale. The fact that Hasegawa filled this large gap in the market will surely revive the modeling business, at least where the airplane part is concerned. This is already noticeable in the release of many new 72nd scale kits in '85. Many of those are released by Hasegawa themselves, of course. Some of these kits are models of airplanes that some of us never expected to see.

VP has taken the chance to fill another gap in the market. Many people seem to have serious problems to simulate the typical airfield tarmac for their diorama. VP have produced cardboard pre-weathered tarmac sections. For starters they come in 72nd scale in two versions, one for general use and one for a heli-pad featuring the large painted H. Yellow tarmac demarcation lines are printed on one side of the A4 size sheets. By cutting and repositioning you can make as large a dispersal as you like. VP are considering to produce these pre-fab sections on 48th scale as well, should the 72nd scale sheets prove to be succesful.

This section shows you just one example of the numerous possibilities the Hasegawa ground equipment and the VP tarmac sections offer. It illustrates the things to do and not to do when displaying an aircraft on the dispersal with a particular sort of action going on.

To illustrate the use of the airfield equipment I chose to display the AC-130 Gunship from Italeri. It is worthwhile to take a closer look at it. I built it as soon as it was released, but never incorporated it into a diorama, precisely because of the lack of equipment.

As you can take from the pictures, I did quite a super-detailing job on the model. I felt it to be an absolute must, since I wanted to sport the model with the ramp and some of the doors opened.

Most of the detail you see is plastic stock and a large selection of spare parts from the scrapbox. Just a few of the small items were specially fabricated. The large items like the radar cabin and ammo and flare racks were all scratchbuilt. There was not too much good documentation on interior details of the AC-130, just a few black & white pictures and sketches in an IPMS/USA Quarterly publication. A lot of the detail shown on the pictures is still guesswork. In general this is not too much of a problem, since nobody is going to check on the detail anyway. The looks are quite convincing, and that is what really counts.

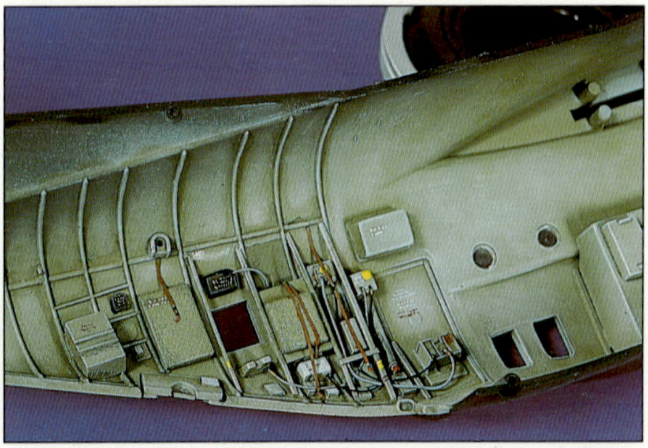

For instance, no matter how great the rush, an aircraft will never be refuelled and rearmed at the same time. This would concentrate too large an amount of explosives in too small an area. You will neither see any kind of equipment that may produce sparks, working in the vicinity of an aircraft that is being refuelled. Nor will any equipment that gives of any kind of radiation, like for instance an aircraft radar, radios or similar, be working in the refuelling/rearming pit. Radiation can be intense enough to trigger an explosion of fuel or bombs and alike. To give you an idea: the microwaves produced by the radar of the E-3A Sentry AWACS will set off anything explosive within a radius of three miles. What's more, it will kill anyone who gets too close.

These are just a few examples. Other aspects to pay attention to are airfield lighting, the position of the parked aircraft, the position of equipment close to an aircraft that is supposed to be cranking its engines and so on. Many things to take into account and many good reasons to double-check on your documentation to make sure that you get all items right in order to display a particular situation.

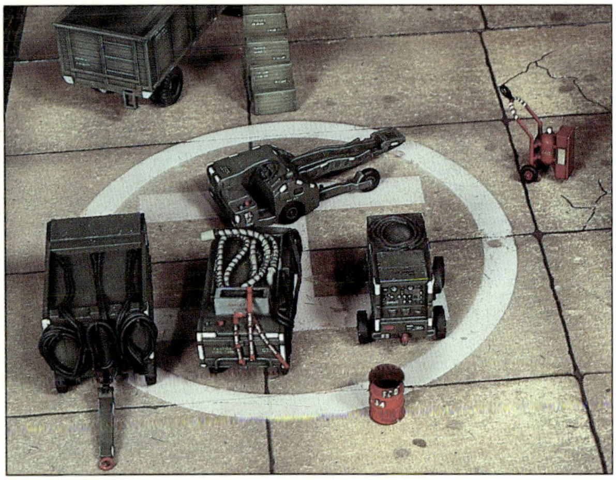

The pictures on this page illustrate the effective use of the Hasegawa ground equipment set. You may use all vehicles on one diorama or just some of them. Very often gear that is not in use is parked on the dispersal itself, waiting for the next plane they have to serve. In this case the generators and hydraulic test vehicle are not in use, while the ground cooling cart has just been unhooked. It should be noted that the large open trailer and fork-lift are not included in any of the Hasegawa sets.

Phantom servants

This second example shows the latest release from Hasegawa in their 72nd scale range of airfield accessories at the time this book was prepared for the printshop. It is combined with some of their earlier weapon and vehicle sets.

The latest set concerns figurines of pilots, groundcrew and air force police. Also featured are a Chevy van, plus some fire extinguishers and work platform.

The figurines are beautifully sculpted and allow you to make a choice of many situations you may encounter on any air base. A nice detail is that Hasegawa did not forget to include some female personnel. More and more women take over non-combatant jobs in many air forces, not only because men are no longer interested in an air force carreer, but very much because women are a lot better in certain jobs than men.

The Chevy utility van is the workhorse of the USAF. It hauls personnel, spare parts and food all around base. The metal piping making up some parts of the fire extinguisher and work platform is a bit on the heavy side. The more experienced modeler may want to replace it by thinner rod.

Painting of the figurines is a little different from painting 35 scale figures, because of their size. Keep it simple by just applying the shades. You cannot and should not go into too much detail. When looking at a 72 scale figurine from a distance of about a foot, it is like looking at a real person

Overall top view of the action on and around the Phantom. Two members of the air force police are looking on, while a groundcrew member is waiting to hook up the external power supply. Another one is walking towards the work platform to move it away out of the jetblast area.

continued from page 55

at over 100 yards away. Just check in the street how much detail you see at that distance. You can hardly make out the white of the eyes.

Placing figurines correctly on an aircraft diorama is just as important as placing the ground equipment correctly. It is beyond the scope of this book to write a complete essay on activities on air bases, we suggest that you check on the many pictures available in books and magazines to get an idea what you can and cannot depict on an aircraft diorama.

By the way, the F-4E is from the new 72nd scale Phantom range from Fujimi.

While the backseater is climbing the ladder, the crewchief stands on the intake, waiting to strap him in. The pilot will be the next one to step into the aircraft.

THE GUNS OF SACRAMENTO

GEOFFREY & DAVID ALLEN

Robin Garton
LONDON · MCMLXXVIII

ISBN 0 906030 06 4

First published 1978 by Robin Garton Ltd.
9 Lancashire Court, New Bond Street, London, W1
Tel. 01-493 2820

Produced by
Richmond-Davies & Associates Ltd., London, WC2
and printed in England by
Gem Graphic Services, Didcot, Oxfordshire

The authors wish to thank the following people for their assistance and encouragement in piecing together the history of this remarkable naval adventure:

Professor C. R. Boxer without whose help and generous co-operation much of the detail would never have been unearthed; the Port Elizabeth Historical Society; The Port Elizabeth Museum; and Mr. Alfred Porter of the Port Elizabeth Library. They would also like to acknowledge the organisational and legal help which they received from Mr. Eric de Villiers, the illustrative drawings done by David Wratten and the editorial work done by Arthur Astbury.

BIBLIOGRAPHY

Diary of Bento Teyzeyra Feyo
Macao and its Diocese volume 9 by Father Manuel Teixeira, Macao, 1969.
Portuguese and Dutch in South Africa 1641–1806 by Sidney R. Welch, Juta, Cape Town.
Panorama of Port Elizabeth by Eleanor K. Lorimer, A. A. Balkema, Cape Town, 1971.
The Harraway papers in the Port Elizabeth Museum files.
Roteiro da Africa do Sul e sueste desde o cabo da boa esperanca ate ao das Correntes (1576) by Manuel de Mesquita Perestrelo annotated by Fontoura da Costa, Agencia Geral das colonais, Lisbon, 1939.

1. *Macau 300 years ago* by Professor C. R. Boxer, Macau Imprensa Nacional, 1942.
   Tower of London Catalogue of Ordnance.
2. *The Great Ship; fidalgos in the Far East 1550–1770* by Professor C. R. Boxer, The Hague, 1948.
   Colonel R. J. Gordon's notes to map 42 of his collection in the Rijksmuseum, Amsterdam.
3. *The Portuguese Missions in Malacca and Singapore (1511–1958), Vol. II Malacca,* Lisbon 1961: "Notes regarding a cannon from Macao at present in the Tower of London" by Dr K. C. Crucq.
   Grande Enciclopedia Portuguese Brasileira.
   Correspondence from Professor C. R. Boxer quoting extracts from his extensive library in Little Gaddesden.
   Asian Potentates and European Artillery in the 16th–18th centuries: a footnote to Gibson-Hill by Professor C. R. Boxer, The Journal of the Malaysian Branch of the Royal Asian Society (Singapore) volume 38 part II, 1966.
   Library files of the *Eastern Province Herald* and *Evening Post,* Port Elizabeth, South Africa.
   Log books and diving records of David Allen and Gerry van Niekerk.
4. *Lloyd's Log* October 1973
   Lloyd's of London damage report on ship *Neptune Sapphire.*
   The Portuguese Seaboard Empire 1415–1825 by Professor C. R. Boxer
   Da navegacao Portuguela no Indico no seculo XVII by Alberto Iria, Lisbon, 1963.

Chapter 1

The saga of the wrecking of the seventeenth-century galleon *Sacramento* with her cargo of Chinese bronze and iron cannon off the coast of South Africa is one of the greatest sea stories of all time. Bound for Portugal, the *Sacramento*, built of teak and fitted to carry sixty cannon, was one of the largest ships of her time: and had she survived her maiden voyage in 1647 she and her consort, the *Atalaya*, which also went down on that dangerous coast, might well have altered the naval fortunes of the Portuguese for the better.

The story of the survivors' long and arduous trek of a thousand miles to safety is only equalled in drama by that of how David Allen discovered the wreck and salvaged forty of its guns three centuries later. Both are told in this book.

The *Sacramento* foundered in 1647 in one of the most dangerous seas in the world, that between Durban and Port Elizabeth on the south-eastern coast of Africa. Not only are gales frequent here in winter, but a hazard is encountered largely unknown elsewhere – freak waves up to sixty feet high which have before now sunk great ships without trace.

The treachery of this stretch of water has been brought home many times in this century. Two or three modern instances will serve to demonstrate the danger into which Portuguese seventeenth century sailors cast themselves when making a passage to and from the Far East.

In 1910 the liner *Waratah* (9,339 tons) was lost without trace off the Bashee River. In 1973 the merchant ship *Neptune Sapphire* (15,501 tons) making a maiden voyage had her entire forepeak severed by the continuous pounding of the sea off Port St John, in the same area as that in which the *Sacramento* went down. Two messages finally relayed to London give a picture of what seemed at the time to be the last hours of this vessel: *Following SOS message received by local radio: motor vessel Neptune Sapphire. Ship sinking due to hole in ship side. Lost bow and number one hatch. Ships in vicinity please stand by us.* A later message read: *Bow section of Neptune Sapphire estimated 200 feet long approximately six foot free-board sighted.* But the *Neptune Sapphire* was eventually towed away stern first for the refitting of a new bow section in Finland, and is still in use.

A final example of the savage power of the sea in the Eastern Cape area concerns the 132,700 ton super-tanker *Wilstar*. Fully laden with 12,600 tons of oil for Europe, she was struck in May 1974 by a freak wave in almost the same latitude.

Her master, Captain Andrzej Janiszewski, describing the storm which carried away the *Wilstar*'s bulbous bow, a forward compartment of 7,000 tons capacity, and caused heavy deck damage with twisted piping and rails all along the forepeak, said that the storm hit them on May 16 and slowed the ship almost to a stop. He stood on the port bridge wing watching the weather deteriorate. The waves were already big and confused, and he had been forced to change into dry uniform three times during the day. "We were going very slowly just inside the hundred fathom line, seventy-nine miles from Durban," he said later. An hour after lunch he was on the bridge wing counting the wave sequence, knowing that every seventh wave is usually bigger than its predecessors. But there was, on this particular occasion, no seventh wave. "Instead," he went on, "we plunged into a huge, dark hole in the sea with a mountain of water piling up over the bow. The sound of the wind dropped. There was only the noise of water falling away from the bows into a large, bottomless abyss. Then the wave piled up on the far side came straight down on the ship's bows – thousands of tons of water crashing on the deck. It was as if we had hit a mountain. The green sea which poured along the long deck smashed against the bridge structure and up and even over the high funnel, finally crashed down on the pool deck in the ship's stern. The ship stopped dead; wallowed in a strange, almost uncanny way; it took half-an-hour to put about."*

It was into these seas that the *Sacramento* and *Atalaya* sailed from theEast over three centuries ago. But in order to understand the immediate impact and the long-term significance of their sinking it is necessary to have a general idea of how Portugal became for a period the world's greatest colonial power; and also how that power developed and centred in Goa and Macao.

The Portuguese empire is the oldest colonial empire in the world. Overseas expansion began during the reign of John I (1385–1433) who married the daughter of John of Gaunt; and in the fifteenth and sixteenth centuries the discoveries of Portuguese navigators made Portugal the greatest maritime nation of its day.

Henry the Navigator, son of John I, and his captains explored the west coast of Africa, discovered Madeira and the Azores (1442), Senegal (1445) and Cape Verde (1446). The Cape of Good Hope was doubled by Bartholomew Dias in 1486, and Vasco da Gama reached India in 1497. In 1500 Portuguese settlements were made in Brazil and, within the next ten years, in Mozambique on the east coast of Africa. Goa, on the west coast of India, was conquered in 1510; and Malacca, on the south-west coast of the Malay Peninsula, in 1511.

Commercial relations were entered into with China in 1517, and with Japan in 1542, Portuguese merchants settling at Macao on the south China coast as early as 1557.

At this time Portugal was at the height of her power and enjoyed a monopoly of the southern and eastern seas, Lisbon being the European centre for trade with the East and Far East.

Decline began in the second half of the sixteenth century, and from 1581 to 1640 Portugal was under the suzerainty of Spain. Some of her possessions in South America and the Malay Archipelago were also seized by England and Holland, although it was not until 1822 that her colony of Brazil obtained complete independence.

When in 1487 Bartholomew Dias rounded Cape Agulhas and sailed into the frightening waters to the east of the southern tip of Africa he was the first Portuguese navigator to do so. He thereby established that there was a sea route to the Far East.

Portuguese navigation was then highly developed by the standards of the time, but there was still a pause before Vasco da Gama, under the orders of King Manuel I, sailed in 1497 to complete the voyage to India. He reached Calicut on its south-west coast in 1498 and returned to Lisbon in July 1499, declaring the route to India with its fabulous spice and jewel trade to be open.

It is suggested by Professor C.R. Boxer in his book *The Portuguese Seaboard Empire 1415–1825*, that the delay between the voyage of Dias and that of da Gama resulted from the fact that the Portuguese navigators spent the intervening years making secret voyages well out into the Atlantic, so that when da Gama set out for India he unhesitatingly took the "great circle" route, and sailed across the Atlantic almost to Brazil before turning to cross the South Atlantic for the

***Lloyd's Log*, in its October 1973 issue, explained the formation of the waves in this way. "The waves usually occur when a local depression produces strong south-westerly winds which generate waves seven to eight metres in height and 60 to 90 metres in length. These waves may be augmented by swell waves of greater length generated from a storm centred some distance southward of the area, with both sets of waves moving in a north-easterly direction against the Agulhas current which runs parallel to the coast.

"Under such conditions when the crests of the sea and swell waves coincide, a steep-fronted wave of exceptional height may occur. Such a wave, which is preceded by a deep trough, may attain a height of 20 metres or more. The crest of such a wave only extends over a short distance and the height is maintained only for as long as the sea and swell waves are in coincidence . . .

"For a vessel encountering such conditions, the effects are sudden and dramatic. A ship riding head-on into the swell will take a sudden bow-dive as the superimposed wave scoops out a trough twice as deep as the one formed by the swell. Almost simultaneously, a wave twice as high as a normal roller breaks on the vessel with terrific impact."

Cape, running before the south-east trade winds. Boxer argues that he would not have dared to use this route unless it had already been well explored.

While the standard of Portuguese navigation was advanced for the time, it is still true to say that throughout their venturing into the Indian and South Atlantic oceans the Portuguese had to rely a good deal on guesswork and good luck because of a lack of accurate charts and other factors. Thus while there were Portuguese settlements in Mozambique within a year or two of 1500, it was not until 1576 that a chart of any consequence of the south-east African coast was drawn – by Manuel de Mesquita Perestrelo, who at the same time provided a roteiro, or series of sailing instructions, for King Sebastian after having been shipwrecked on the coast of Africa. Indeed one pilot, Aleixo da Mota, a veteran of the *Carreira da India*, or round voyage to and from India from Lisbon, warned: "Throughout this course from the tip of the island Sao Lourenco (Madagascar) to the line (equator) you must navigate with great care by day and night; remembering that the latitudes of the shoals and islands are not always accurately marked at all. Therefore keep a man at the masthead by day and watch for changes in the colour of the sea. And at night station a man on the bowsprit, keep casting the lead, and reduce sail; trusting only in God and in the good lookout you must keep."

It is interesting, in this connection, to read the comments of Sir Richard Hawkins, the English seaman, on Portuguese navigators. They are contained in his *Observations* published in 1622. "In this point of steeridge, the Spaniards and Portuguese do exceed all that I have seen, I mean for their care, which is chiefest in navigation. And I wish in this, and in all their works of discipline and reformation, we should follow their example . . . In every ship of moment, upon the halfdeck, or quarterdeck, they have a chair or seat out of which, whilst they navigate, the pilot, or his adjutants (which are the same officers which in our ships we term the master and his mates) never depart, day or night, from the sight of the compass; and have another before them; whereby they see what they do, and are ever witness of the good or bad steeridge of all men that do take the helm."

But in spite of their achievements, the Portuguese navigators had other handicaps to overcome apart from unreliable charts, or no charts at all. The problems were many: there was scant regard for hygiene aboard the ships, and a large percentage of each crew could be expected to die on every voyage; the men were ill-paid and frequently cheated by the merchants and captains; they were badly used, with all consideration going to officers or passengers prepared to pay for comfortable accommodation; and in Portugal seamen were regarded as being the lowest social order. At times the situation was almost desperate, with hardly enough men in India to man one ship for a return voyage to Lisbon. A report from Goa in 1558 put the total number of seamen in India at 400, only enough to man two or three ships at most. In consequence, as the Portuguese developed colonies in West Africa and Mozambique, they tended to use black slaves in increasing numbers aboard their ships. It was often the blacks who mastered the seaman's craft rather than the Portuguese sailors, some of whom survived a lifetime at sea without learning to read a compass or to sail a ship with any degree of competence. In moments of adversity the white crew, captain and all, would turn to prayer rather than attempt to save the ship; and Boxer says it was most common to abandon the ship to God and gather to pray – often on the poop deck – where the priests who frequently took passage would bless each wave lest it swamp the ship. It is Boxer's opinion that perhaps dozens of ships were lost needlessly in this way. In fact what sustained the Portuguese voyages of discovery was the excellence of a handful of pilots and captains, who despite the difficulties of finding competent crew were themselves able to perform remarkable feats of navigation.

Chapter 2

The three main Portuguese ports in India were Goa, Calicut and Cochin, all on the south-west coast, and a flourishing trade soon developed between them and Lisbon.

Golden Goa, as it was called, was captured by Alfonso de Albuquerque in 1510 from the Sultan of Bijapur, and became the main entrepot port for goods from China and Japan as well as from the islands of the Pacific. Goa, and more particularly the town of Bassein some 300 or more miles farther north along the same coast, rapidly became centres of Portuguese ship-building because the teak which grew there was superior to the pine being used in Portugal. Ships built of pine in Portugal had to be sheathed in lead below the water line, an expensive operation which had to be repeated at regular intervals to prevent the entry of wood or toredo worm in the pine making the ships unseaworthy. There were no such problems in India. A royal order of 1585 declared ". . . experience has shown that those which are built there (India) last much longer than those built in this Kingdom, as also they are cheaper and stronger, and . . . suitable timber for these carracks (galleons) is increasingly hard to get here." In fact a leading naval architect of the period remarked, "Teak is incorruptible and seems fashioned by nature for naval architects."

But Portugal's advance into the East did not go unchecked. Holland and England were equally determined to profit from the riches there, and with the unification of the Portuguese and Spanish thrones under Philip II of Spain in 1580, when Portugal became involved in the wars in the Netherlands and Germany, the Dutch declared war on the Portuguese possessions in Asia. Used to war, well armed, and with disciplined crews, the Dutch ships in the Indian Ocean were able to harass, capture and sink Portuguese merchantmen almost at will. More important, they were able to mount a continuous blockade of the strategically important peninsula of Macao – *The City of the Name of God in China* as Antonio Bocarro, official Portuguese chronicler in India, had it.

Macao was important to the Portuguese for two reasons: her merchants conducted a valuable carrying trade between China and Japan; and it contained the foundry in which the world's finest guns were made. So essential to our story are the foundry at Macao and the guns it produced that we must now deal with them both, and with the city itself, in some detail.

Macao, ultimately at the heart of Portugal's far eastern trading empire, began as a fishing village on a tiny peninsula, linked to the mainland by a causeway. It was developed as a trading port by the Portuguese under an agreement made in 1557 with the Mandarin of Canton. The existence of the agreement was discovered twenty years later by the Emperor in Peking, who reluctantly sanctioned the arrangement. In 1585 the Portuguese Viceroy of India proclaimed Macao a city. It was then a vibrant, commercial place of 40,000 people. There were noblemen, merchant adventurers, hangers-on to the rich, seamen, soldiers, swashbucklers, and slaves. They were people to whom commerce was second nature, who quickly saw that they could make a better living there by exploiting the long running political tension between Japan and China, and acting as commercial carriers between the two, than by relying on the rewards of the long haul to Lisbon.

They were merchants keen to cook the books, bribe an official here, an assessor there, rig the bills of lading, and cheat the king of his proportion of the proceeds of their efforts. It was a city of delightfully devious men maintaining a precarious relationship with their Chinese hosts, who frequently had reason to regret ever allowing them to settle, and who as frequently imposed economic sanctions on the peninsula city to teach the wayward inhabitants a lesson over some more than usually outrageous incident. The chronicler Antonio Bocarro wrote in his contemporary description of the city in 1635, "This city is not so well furnished with food supplies, of which many both good and cheap are available in the interior, because we obtain them from the Chinese, when they have any dispute with us they immediately deprive us of them, without those citizens (of Macao) having any means of going to fetch them elsewhere." At such times the narrow entrance through the wall which the Portuguese had built across the peninsula served the Chinese as much in their efforts to withhold food as it did the citizens of Macao when occasionally they wished to keep the Chinese out of the city.

Bocarro wrote that there were 850 Portuguese families with their slaves in the town, and as many Chinese families. "Besides these this city contains many Portuguese sailors, pilots and masters, the majority of them married in the Kingdom (Portugal) whilst others are bachelors who sail in the voyages to Japan, Manila, Solor, Macassar, and Cochin-China. There are over 150 of these, some of them very wealthy, with capital of over 50,000 xerafins, and who are resolved never to go to Goa, lest they may be seized by the justices for some offence or by the Viceroys for His Majesty's service. There are also many rich unmarried merchants, to whom the same reason applies." (Bocarro does not mention it, but in this far-flung place they also avoided the attention of the Inquisition.) These were men who were prepared to seize every opportunity to advance their own position; who reached zeniths of power only to be cut down again, often hilariously, by the machinations of their enemies. In the name of the King, comfortably out of touch half a world away, they set spies to work, laid plots, murdered and intrigued; but above all they made money.

They spent it too, as was made clear by an envious Dutch visitor to Nagasaki in 1610 who described the arrival there of a typical merchant ship from Macao. "It usually has about 200 merchants aboard who go ashore at once, each of them taking a house wherein to lodge with his servants and slaves. They take no heed of what they spend and nothing is too costly for them."

In their trading the merchants took raw and manufactured silks as well as gold from China to exchange for silver bullion from Japan. The Japanese coveted the quality of the Chinese silks while the Chinese required high quality silver. From Japan, too, they bought large quantities of copper, most of which was sent on via Macao and Goa to Portugal, whence it flooded the European market, forced a fall in price, and nearly ruined the Scandinavian copper trade.

Another description of Macao, and of its fortifications, comes down to us from the Italian, Marco d'Avalo, who wrote in 1638, "The island was granted by the Mandarins of Canton to the Portuguese so that they could build a town . . . The said city lies encircled by walls and ramparts, and has three hills situated in the manner of a triangle. The best and strongest of the castles is called Saint Paulo where the general Antonio de Mascarenhas, resided; it has thirty-four cannon all of bronze, the least of which fires an iron ball weighing thirty-four pounds. The second fort is called Nostra Seignora de la Penna de Francis, and contains within its walls a barrage of the same invocation, it has six light guns with iron shot of six to eight pounds. The third fort called Nostra Seignora de Guyll, lies outside the town and is of no use, except in so far that this hill being higher than the others overlooks them, whence it is fortified and provided with four or five cannon. It has likewise a hermitage within its walls.

"From the said hill and fort, the city is appraised by means of bell ringing whenever any vessel from Japan, Manila, or from the north or south thereof is sighted or seen. Likewise when any sail is sighted from fort or hill of Nostra Seignora the bells thereof are rung. Furthermore the city also has three bulwarks on the ground, whereof three are on the sea or water side and four on the land side. The first is called the bulwark of Santiago de la Barra, whereby the ships pass and which is very fine and strong, having the appearance of a small town in itself when seen from afar, owing to the large building and soldiers' barracks in its circuit. There is a redoubt on the hill top above it serving as a refuge, wherein are 16 heavy guns, whereof four have very wide mouths for shooting stones, whilst the rest are of 24 pound iron shot calibre. Within this aforesaid bulwark there is another and higher bastion, provided with six cannon like the foregoing, which have a very long range.

"All ships and junks which wish to enter this bar or harbour, must necessarily pass within three or four pikes' lengths of this fort, because the Portuguese have blocked the remaining channels in order to protect the place better."

Today Macao is only the shadow of its glorious past. The city is run down and unattractive, and the communist influence of the mainland strong among the inhabitants. But to the last it has retained that spark of financial adventure on which its greatness was based. Macao is now a miniature Las Vegas, with tourists flocking there by high-speed hydrofoil from Hong Kong to gamble in the casino and watch their money flit past the winning post on the new race course; but of the three million visitors who landed there in 1977 and hurried to change their money into multi-coloured gambling chips, few can have had in mind the glorious history of *The City of the Name of God in China*.

During Macao's former days of glory, a foundry was established in 1623 on the orders of the city's first Captain-General, Dom Francisco Mascarenhas. Mascarenhas had been sent to the city on the orders of the Viceroy of India in 1622 when the citizens requested protection after a Dutch raid had only just been beaten off. It was Mascarenhas who restored the city walls as the main form of protection: the guns were useful, but were intended primarily for export, and mainly to India.

But the city was well suited for gun production. There was ample iron from the mines of China, and high grade copper for use in bronze guns was available from Japan. Furthermore the Chinese were well versed in the manufacture of gunpowder and already had a working knowledge of casting cannon, though European guns were regarded throughout the East as far superior to locally cast pieces.

The first contract to produce guns at the foundry was awarded by Mascarenhas to "Quinqo and Haizon, two long-haired heathen Chinese", who signed the articles in October 1623. It seems that they cast iron guns only, while the Portuguese founders who arrived later cast the bronze cannon. They were soon replaced by Manuel Tavares Bocarro, the Eurasian grandson of Francisco Dias Bocarro, master founder at Goa until 1587 when his son Pedro Dias Bocarro was appointed in his place. (The family had no connection with the chronicler Antonio Bocarro.) Pedro continued to use Chinese lakom almost exclusively and the products of the foundry soon outstripped those of Goa in quality. Indeed Manuel made the Macao foundry the best in the world, and all the Portuguese forts in the Orient were equipped with guns made there.

Seventeenth century accounts of Macao are crammed with proud references to Bocarro's foundry. Father Manuel Teixeira, a Jesuit priest living in Macao, quoting a source dated 1655, wrote "This city beats all others in large cannon for a reasonable price and they do considerable business as they are considered the best in all India, being forged with Chinese and Japanese copper and sent far and wide." In 1635 the chronicler Bocarro wrote "Altogether there are seventy-three pieces of artillery in the city of Macao, apart from many iron guns which are being cast for private individuals as well as on the King's account. For this place has one of the best gun-foundries in the world, whether of bronze, which it has had long since, or of iron, which was made by order of the Viceroy, Conde de Linhares, and where artillery is being cast continually for the whole of this state (India) at a very reasonable price; which is what it most needs, and whence it could be entirely supplied if the strait of Singapore was open instead of being continually blockaded by the Hollanders during the monsoon, as has been stated previously." In another passage Bocarro tells of frequent naval skirmishes in which the Portuguese almost always triumphed because their ships were armed with Bocarro cannon. "The Portuguese always come off best, for since those of Macao are wealthy and not lacking in artillery, their pinnaces are very well found." The contemporary Italian chronicler Marco d'Avalo was not so lavish in his praise, noting only "There is furthermore a gun-foundry here, where fine cannon are cast annually, both of bronze and iron."

For almost a century, between 1580 and 1680, gun-founding both in Goa and Macao was dominated by the Bocarro family – not only by the beautifully ornate bronze guns and exceptionally sound iron guns for which they were famous, but also small arms, ammunition, and even bells. The younger Bocarro attained the height of his craft in Macao and his guns, as well as those of his father, were eagerly sought by every potentate in the East. They were not only regarded as fine machines of war but also as status symbols with magical religious powers. Thus in 1638 the Viceroy in Goa wrote to Lisbon stating that the king of Macassar had asked to be allowed to have cannon cast in Macao at his own expense. Japanese and Chinese potentates frequently used Bocarro cannon against one another, and in the dying years of the Ming dynasty Bocarro cannon, and gunners trained in Macao, were often used in battles against the invading Manchus. As late as 1841 a Bocarro cannon was captured by the English in Kwangtung province during the Opium War and sent to be preserved at the Tower of London.

Bocarro's genius lay in founding cheap and easily turned out iron guns which did not shatter, or blow apart killing the gunners. By contrast his bronze cannon were by any standards exquisite works of art, with elaborate markings and ornamentation. Each cannon was named after a saint, inscribed and engraved with elaborate work and crest. Each cannon also had slightly oriental "lifting dolphins" worked in some detail – shackles in the shape of leaping dolphins by which they could be slung and placed in position aboard ship or in a fortress. Lower down the barrel was the crest of Macao, two cherubs, one on each side of a globe with the cross of Christ. Below this was the lion and crown crest of thee Governor of India – in the case of the *Sacramento* cannon, that of Antonio Telles de Menezese – which stood slightly above an ornate inscription bearing the order for the cannon to be cast, and the date when this was done. The gunsmith's name, surrounded by ornate oriental faces and cloves of pepper, was just below the touch-hole, and each cannon had an elaborate cascabel – the end piece behind the base-ring either in the form of a clenched fist with the thumb protruding between the fingers, or a lotus bud. These served as fertility symbols or as guardians against the evil eye. It was largely these fertility symbols which gave the cannon their sacro-magical qualities; in India, in particular, they were often bought for this reason alone. A woman unable to conceive would rub herself against the thumb to increase her chances of giving birth.

Little is known about Bocarro's private life, although it is known that he was married in Macao and by 1642 was considered a "local" man, being appointed Captain-General in 1657 and holding that post until 1664. It seems that his foundry began to decline when his ready supply of copper was cut by the ending of the trade with Japan. Boxer also thinks it unlikely that he would have continued as master founder while he held office as Captain-General. No definite date is known for the closing of the foundry and cannon were certainly produced in Macao until

1680, though by then its reputation as the foremost gun founding centre in the East had long since passed. And until the discovery of the *Sacramento* only a handful of cannon from the prolific output of his foundry, and a few bells, of which one still hangs in the church of St Lawrence in Macao, remained as testimony to Bocarro's outstanding abilities. The foundry no longer exists.

We must now return to the period when Portugal and her overseas possessions were under attack by the Dutch, and Macao itself under blockade. So important was the foundry to Portugal, and so valuable was its growing stockpile of bronze and iron weapons – which because of the Dutch blockade could reach the outside world in little more than a trickle – that it was essential for Lisbon to retain control of Macao. But if an attempt was made to move the heavy and cumbersome cannon it would be necessary to have a bigger ship than those used to run the Dutch blockade. One such attempt was successfully made in 1635 when the Portuguese Viceroy in India hired the English ship *London*, commanded by Captain Wills, to bring the first important cargo of Macao cannon as well as copper and other merchandise to India, on the correct assumption that the Dutch would not attack a neutral bottom. Although the Dutch knew that the vessel was carrying a strategic cargo on her outward journey – several tons of iron to be founded into cannon – and that cannon were being carried on the return journey, the Dutch let the ship through the blockade on both occasions.

In February of the next year the Manager of the Voyages to Japan as he was known, Manuel Ramos, wrote to the Viceroy in India "The founder Manuel Tavares Bocarro is continuing with his iron foundry, and has 45 pieces ready. I hope that until April when he can work only in the ministry because of the weather, he has 70 to 80, if the Chinese do not run short of iron; these are much better than those that went on the English ship and he applies himself in the manner whch is very worthy of the big honours and rewards."

Two years later three ships under the command of Captain Weddell, carrying similar cargoes to those of the *London* and under the same sort of agreement, were also let through the blockade. They were the last Bocarro cannon to be carried to India in this way. In January 1641 the Dutch captured the English ship *Bonne Esperance* and no further ships were hired to the Portuguese.

On the restoration of John IV to the throne of Portugal in 1640, the factors affecting Portuguese foreign policy became more complex, and the need to secure the Bocarro cannon more urgent.

In the previous year the Japanese dynasty had banned the Portuguese trade with China (by ordering that any Portuguese ships which entered Japanese ports might be captured) and had given the monopoly to the Dutch. Macao, almost wholly financially dependent on that trade, then turned to Spanish Manila as the alternative. But with the end of Spanish suzerainty in 1640, Portugal and Spain found themselves no longer allies, but enemies. It therefore became essential for the Portuguese government to secure the cannon, and for two reasons: first to prevent their falling into Spanish hands if the Macao merchants switched allegiance; and secondly so they could be brought to Portugal to use against the Spanish enemy.

On his accession, King John, mindful of the need to ensure the continued loyalty of Macao and to protect his own rights to the magnificent arsenal of Bocarro cannon, sent an ambassador to the Far East the moment his throne was secured. His ambassador, Antonio Fialho Ferreira, had a long voyage and one interrupted by innumerable improbable adventures; and it was not until November 1643 that he was able to send a letter ahead from the island of St Helena to say that he was on his way back, and that the loyalty of Macao had been secured.

In the meantime other efforts were being made by the King's advisors to ensure the safety of the cannon. Thus when news of King John's accession reached him at Goa in September 1641, the Procurator-General of Japan, Father Antonio Francisco Cardim of the Society of Jesus, was desperately worried that Macao must be secured, if necessary by force, and the cannon already stockpiled there moved to safety. He therefore sought an urgent audience with the new Viceroy, Count de Aveiras, in order to hand over a letter for the king. The letter, together with a lengthy addendum, was considered by the Exchequer Court in Lisbon in December 1642.

Father Cardim wrote in part: "I went to speak with the Count de Aveiras, Viceroy of the State of India, and gave him a memorial (memorandum) pointing out the need of sending special advice to the City of Macao concerning the favour God had shown us in restoring Your Majesty to his kingdoms, so that the inhabitants of Macao should swear loyalty and obedience to him as in the other cities of India and that they should not take goods to the Spaniards in Manila, as they usually do yearly to the amount of two million in gold. For if this news should arrive late, after the Portuguese and their goods were already in Manila, there would be a danger of Macao choosing the side of the King of Spain, owing to there being too involved with the Spaniards in Manila wherein were so many of their people and goods."

Impressed by Cardim's argument, the Viceroy had already undertaken to send a ship to Macao on his own initiative, but the plan was later abandoned. Meanwhile it became known in Goa that Ferreira was wintering in Bantam (in Indonesia) and could well be inordinately delayed in getting to Macao.

Cardim pointed out these problems in his letter, and continued "To remedy these evils I present Your Majesty a memorial dated October 5 in which I showed that it was necessary for Your Majesty to send two pinnaces or caravels directly from this court (Goa) to Macao, which ought to be done in January, as this will give them time to catch the monsoon in the Straits of Sunda, saving them from wintering in Bantam as happened to Antonio Fialho (Ferreira)." Cardim said there was no naval force in Macao to oppose the king's ships if the city had already switched loyalties, and added, "In the event of the city of Macao being lost, which God forbid, Your Majesty will lose the best trade in India, nor can India be rich without China."

In his closing paragraphs Father Cardim turned his attention to the Bocarro cannon. "If Your Majesty sends ships directly to Macao, Your Majesty gains that city, the citizens are greatly heartened, and trade is opened with this kingdom, which will be very advantageous to both parties. For from here can be sent anything which is normally sent to Goa, while the return (to Lisbon) is much greater and more profitable, since the numerous cast iron cannon can be sent as ballast, the best in the world, besides much bronze artillery, all very strong and reliable, for that of iron does not burst and at the most only splits without doing hurt. Many thousands of muskets can be sent; munitions; the best ginger in the world, preserved in grated form; powdered dry, or preserved in marmalade form; much benzoin; eagle-wood; calambac; cloves; cinnamon; sandal wood; fine china; all kinds of wrought and raw silks; brocaded stuffs; musk; rubies; pearls; seed-pearls; and many other goods." (Benzoin is an aromatic resin; eagle-wood and calambac are trees containing a resin fragrant in burning.)

In his addendum Cardim highlighted the crucial element in any adventure to save the cannon: ensuring that the ships sailed from Macao at exactly the right time of year to take best advantage of the weather.

He wrote: "I invariably stated in my memorials that it was necessary to leave before the end of January or by the 8th of February at the latest, in order to avoid what happened to Antonio Fialho Ferreira, who through leaving late, lost the monsoon in the Straits of Sunda (via which this voyage must be made) and thus failed to achieve his purpose. It is disadvantageous to winter in Mozambique or Cochin, because it will then be impossible to go to China except in a year from next July. This will involve great expense in wintering eight months, which the ship will be forced to do if it sails to the coast of India. For this reason, as it is now so late in the season, it will be better either not to leave at all or to go by Goa. This is and always was my opinion, writing as one who has sailed those southern seas for 20 years, and passed the Gulf of Hainan nine times. And for as much as there are numerous islands in the south seas, and the shoals are many, it is very dangerous for anyone to go who has had no previous experience thereof. For this reason I have named some persons who have sailed those seas and who have been in the City of Macao."

Father Cardim's sense of urgency was based on his personal knowledge of the roguish nature of the merchants of Macao and their almost total involvement in commerce at the expense of most other values. But he need not have worried, for Ferreira was a wily and ingenious man. He had spent considerable time in Macao and incurred the disfavour of the citizens for his zeal in the name of the Crown, and knew the urgency of his mission. Not the man to be frustrated in his plans by having to winter at Bantam, he sent a secret letter to Macao. The letter was delivered to the Captain-General there after having been sent to Manila, where a ship was bought by Portuguese trading there to send the message to Macao. To Ferreira's delight the citizens of Macao, though deeply dispirited at losing the wealthy Japanese trade, reaffirmed their allegiance, each signing his name in a specially prepared municipal book; and Ferreira was able to assure the king that the cannon were safely secured for Lisbon.

In his letter from St Helena he wrote: "They (the Macanese) showed that they regretted this inability (to send a cargo to Lisbon immediately) more of being thereby deprived of the opportunity of serving Your Majesty rather than by reason of their own private interests, since they were then possessed of two hundred and fifty pieces of admirably cast iron cannon of various calibres, for use both on land and sea, as also more than fifty bronze cannon, firing shot of sixteen to twenty-five thousand round shot of cast iron; eighteen and two thousand quintals* of copper which remain in charge of the founder, and which are being used up continually; a great quantity of powder, many muskets and arquebuses, which are likewise made there, and sold very cheaply albeit they are among the best in the world. Part of all this belongs to Your Majesty's treasury, derived from the profits of the Japanese voyages which were so profitable during these last years. The citizens of Macao were deeply grieved that they could not send all these engines of war to Lisbon forthwith, to participate in the wars which they feel certain and assured Your Majesty must be engaged in."

The inventory of the cannon is testimony to Bocarro's industry. It is also interesting to note that he had stockpiled so much copper that it was possible to continue production well after the end of trading with Japan – it would have been possible to cast at least twenty more major pieces with the copper he had in stock.

Although Ferreira knew, while in the Far East, that the Macanese were willing, and indeed anxious, for guns to be sent to Lisbon, he had no ship big enough to take them. He therefore returned to Europe via St Helena and arrived in Portugal in 1643.

Still determined to bring back for his king as many of the Bocarro cannon as he could, Ferreira seems to have set off back to Macao at once, where he found the Portuguese not only distressed at the ending of the Japanese trade, but also threatened by the Tartar invasion of China. Most of them were for the first time keen to leave.

In order to further his plans the Viceroy of India sent a galleon, the *Saõ Pedro O Grande*, to Macao chiefly to fetch the bronze cannon from the foundry, together with some iron guns. At the end of 1645 Ferreira therefore set sail for the last time from Macao as Captain-Major of a fleet of eight ships including the *Saõ Pedro O Grande* and his own galleon the *Saõ Andre*. His voyage

*The precise meaning of this phrase, and the equivalent weight today, are uncertain. Perhaps something like one hundred tons is meant.

to Goa was as adventurous as anything else in his life, and after a contretemps with the Dutch in Malacca when he refused to salute their flag or pay harbour dues, he brought the treasured cannon to Goa at the end of January 1646.*

At anchor in Goa were two ships ideally suited to bring the guns back to Lisbon: the old, but unusually large galleon, *Nossa Senhora da Atalaya*; and the newly completed, and even bigger galleon, *Sacramento*. The two ships had been ordered to await the arrival of the guns by the Governor, Antonio Telles de Menezese, acting on the orders of the king; and within a month of the arrival of Ferreira's fleet they were transhipped to the *Sacramento* and *Atalaya*.

There then occurred a delay in sailing the reasons for which are not entirely clear. It may reasonably be assumed, however, that the main cause was the need for Ferreira to sort out his difficulties with the Dutch, and then his death before the transfer of the cargo was complete. Other causes of delay were difficulties in getting crew; the sheer work involved in moving one hundred tons of cannon; and probably slackness on the part of the crew combined with protracted farewells.

The timetable seems to be that Ferreira arrived in Goa "at the end of January". His difficulties with the Dutch must have been telescoped into a few days; for he seems to have died in that same month. The guns were loaded "within a month", which suggests that the ships were ready to sail (say) in the last week of February; but were then delayed "almost until the end of February". If these timings are correct the final delay can have been a matter of two or three days only. Yet that delay was to prove fatal to both ships and most of their crews, and bring disaster to the whole expedition. For as Father Cardim pointed out in his letter, the timing of the voyage was vital if the cannon were to be brought safely to Portugal. Both ships were also under orders not to winter in Mozambique, which could double the time of a passage, but to sail without delay to Lisbon. (In discouraging wintering in Mozambique – and what resulted from this general policy, ignoring the Cape of Good Hope as a port – the commercially-minded Portuguese allowed the dictates of commerce to override considerations of safety and health.) But in the event the *Sacramento* and *Atalaya*, by delaying until the end of February, and then spending further time in examining a strange ship near Mozambique, were faced with the prospect of rounding the Cape of Good Hope in winter.

The chronology which may be held to put the blame for disaster on a delay of two or three days is not, however, unrealistic, for Boxer highlights the importance of ships sailing at the correct time of the year between Portugal and India when he quotes a contemporary comment, "The last day of February is time enough, but the first day of March is late."

Atalaya was sailing under foresail and spritsail on the orders of the pilot, Gaspar Rodrigues Coelho, when she made Algoa Bay. The under-pilot, Balthazar Rodrigues, also a ship's officer, was concerned that the ship was too close to land, but the pilot told him he had years of experience in this part of the world and there was nothing to fear. At this point a relation of the pilot, Bras de Costa, who was directing the ship's course from "the top" (a lookout post on the mainmast) shouted to them "Veer off brothers". Comments Feyo, "All were thrown into confusion on seeing themselves upon a shoal which is in the sea off Algoa Bay, in eight fathoms of water, which was found on casting the lead, with what affliction to all, may easily be imagined by those who have endured the like peril."

To those who know the area it is fascinating that Feyo should in this way describe with absolute accuracy the Riybank, an exceptionally dangerous shoal at the eastern edge of Algoa

*Ferreira's claim to have entered Malacca and refused to salute the Dutch flag or pay harbour dues when the Portuguese and Dutch were at war should be considered in the knowledge that he was a genial and unreliable eccentric and that consistency is not a strong feature of his letters.

terra dos fumos
p. dos fumos
p. da pescaria
p. do meio
terra do natal
b. da alagoa
c. das serras
b. fermosa
c. dos baxos

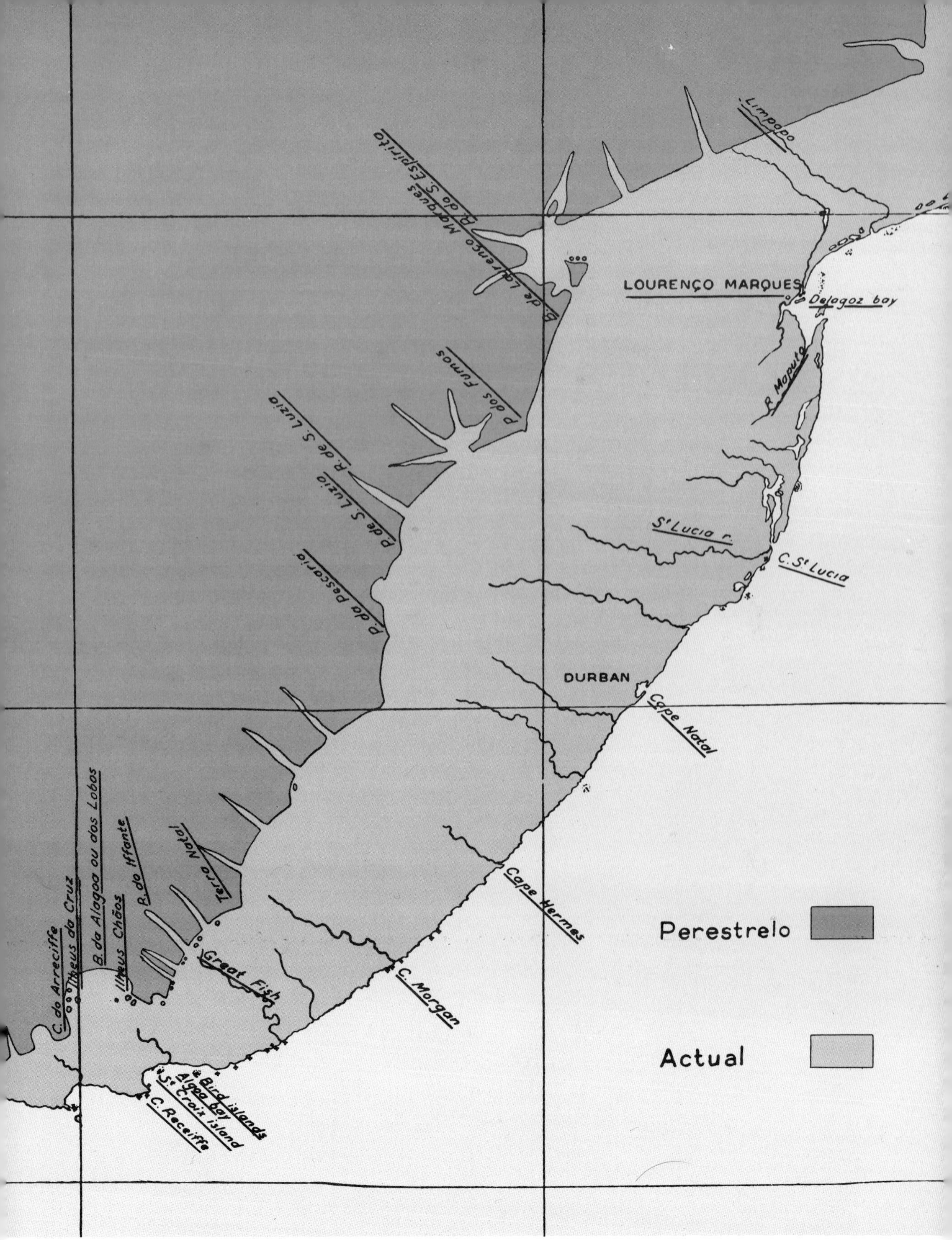

For three hundred years the charts of the eastern coast of Southern Africa were alarmingly inaccurate, showing the land cutting away too quickly to the North. This cartographical error was the cause of many sea disasters. Here the first chart of the area, drawn by Manuel Perestrelo in 1576 is contrasted with the modern chart. The contrast illustrated dramatically how Perestrelo's chart, left, though remarkably accurate for its day, has the land cutting away north too rapidly.

Bay; for while Perestrelo did note it, he dismissed it in his brief comments on Cape Arrecife, now known as Cape Recife. "On the western side (of the point of the cape) there is a flat bank of sand" he writes "and on the low coast some rocks that look like islets, but are not. Between them and the cape there is a shoal near the land . . . On the western side (of Algoa Bay) there are four islets which are called *Of the Cross*, one of them larger than the three around it, where any ship can find shelter at all times for the bottom is clean sand with 12 and 13 fathoms of water." These islets, discovered by Dias and called by him Ilheus de Santa Cruz (Isles of the Holy Cross) still retain the name in the largest of their number, which is known as St Croix Island.

Today the Riybank, while still a dangerous shoal to navigators, is popular with line fishermen – fish feed in the shallow waters and trawlers are unable to put their nets down because the bottom is rocky in some areas. It is marked on charts as having only thirty-six feet of water above it; but the waves, which are always big, can break on the reef in time of storm in spite of the depth of water above it, becoming heaped, confused, and dangerous.

For the pilot to have stumbled over the Riybank shoal when the waves were breaking on the reef shows that the sea must have been running high. When the bank does "break" it is visible even from the shore some distance away; and while the *Atalaya* would be unlikely to come to grief by hitting the bottom, she might have fallen apart in such turbulent seas.

We have seen that according to Perestrelo there was shelter for ships near the island now known as St Croix Island. It is curious that instead of making for it the *Atalaya*, guided by Bras da Costa from his perch on the mainmast, should turn out to sea again once she had cleared the Riybank.

The efforts made to avoid grounding are described by Feyo in the following words. "Speedily we set about unfurling the main topsail, hoisting and hauling it down more than a dozen times, in which officers and all assisted, no one failing in his duty. Then the under-pilot Balthazar Rodrigues, who in this strait never lost his mind, cried from the cross-trees from which he was directing the course, that we should not fear, for he would guide the ship where she could pass, while the waves broke on every side, and the ship laboured in great distress and broaching to pitched three times heavily, at the great shock of which such cries arose that it seemed the world was coming to an end."

Then came a land breeze by which the ship got out to sea again; but the final blow came next day when a great storm arose. The account of the ship's last hours cannot be given better than in Feyo's own words. ". . . the ship was so shaken by this labour that she leaked in every seam. We all took to the pumps, and found the water increase; and a great stòrm which arose next day contributed to this. We sailed with the fore storm-sails, the sea running so high and the ship pitching so heavily that we expected her to part amidships every hour, the waves rising over the lantern and masts, so that the fathers were obliged to relieve each other in the stern every hour and continue blessing the waves, for if they desisted for a moment we were overwhelmed. The under-pilot, who was at the helm, was almost drowned by a wave, and shouted for assistance, being alone, for we were all at the pumps. Our bodily strength was almost gone with the strain of working them, in which the religious and passengers never faltered. Being few, we had the starboard pump under our charge, and the ship boys worked the larboard (port) pump and the Kaffirs the wheel pump. Dom Duarte Lobo and Dom Sebastião Lobo da Silveira were present day and night from the 13th of June, when this work commenced, assisting those who laboured with encouragement and kind words, for as the stove failed us, all this was necessary and nothing sufficed. The wheel-pump gave us great trouble and anxiety, the chain breaking every hour.

"It was ordered that the Kaffirs should work the pumps during the night-watches, but it was not done, and only the two caulkers worked them. Seeing the water increase, they sometimes gave warning of the danger we were in, and they were told not to cause a disturbance in the ship. At daybreak the large hatchway was opened, and the water was found to be above the ballast. Then barrels were diligently prepared to be filled with buckets; but it proved useless, for in less than two hours the water increased so much that with the pitching of the ship the barrels filled of themselves. Then the pipes in the hold and the bales of pepper gradually burst, so that the pumps ceased working altogether, being choked with pepper. At the large hatchway there were only working two barrels of four almudes (a Portuguese unit of capacity) and two of six, which were continually worked with the capstan. Abaft the mainmast, where we opened a hatchway, they worked with two tubs, getting out more pepper than water.

"In this danger the ship's prow sank as if she was broken-backed, she would not obey the helm as before, the water was already over the coamings of the lower hatches and the prow more than two spans deeper than the lower deck. We spent two days and two nights in this imminent peril without seeing land, and then we observed at daybreak the point of a ridge thickly wooded, which appeared to be the mouth of a river with a very long sandy beach, and a great bay where it seemed that we could land with the boat dry-shod.

"It was determined in counsel that on account of the state of the ship we should run her on shore, throwing the artillery into the sea, which was all pointed through the port-holes constantly, except that of Cuina which was in the hold; but this was not done, being beyond our strength, and only two pieces were thrown overboard. With a favourable wind but a rough sea we unfurled the main topsail, which went to pieces as we hoisted it, and so did the fore topsail; and the spritsail was all torn, and the fore-sail had many seams open; then we tried the mainsail, and as we secured it with the tack, fixing a tack-tackle to assist it, it went to pieces.

"At this time the captain had already ordered the gunner, Francisco Teixeira, to put some powder and balls in barrels, and to collect all the arms he could and all the copper and bronze for the maintenance of the camp, as this is the current coin of Kaffraria, that we might trade for what was necessary. The night was spent in working at the buckets, and the Kaffirs were already on shore with great fires alight. The next day, the 3rd of July, in the morning we set about preparing the boat to land some of the people, should the sea permit. The wind rose, and raising the anchor we went ahead with the foresail set, and cast anchor in the bay in seven fathoms. The master ordered the main halliards to be cut, and the yard lay across the middle of the deck, that being cut into pieces it might serve some to get ashore."

A boat's party was sent inshore to see whether they could land, while others of the crew remained on board working the pumps to keep the ship afloat. The boat party returned to say that they did not dare to land because of the breakers and the strength of the current. When night fell the tide went down and the ship began to strike the ground, this loosened the rudder. They therefore chopped down the mainmast and foremast and threw out another anchor to prevent the ship dragging; and when the tide rose again the *Atalaya* floated in forty-eight feet of water.

At daybreak all the thin ropes available were made into a surf-line which was coiled in the boat. The passengers took to the boat with their arms and whatever they could carry. Leaving one end of the surf-line made fast aboard the *Atalaya*, they rowed towards the shore. When they reached the breakers the surf was so turbulent that the father friar on board gave everyone absolution because of the danger.

The party landed without opposition from the Kaffirs, put their belongings on shore, and returned to the ship. A second time the boat made the trip to shore bringing back two Portuguese women, all the negresses who had been on board the ship, the captain Dom

Sebastião Lobo and others.

The boat made four trips to the shore, and in the last Dom Duarte Lobo, his officers, and others to a total number of seventy, were landed after a dangerous passage in which although some were swimming, the boat was sunk to the gunwales. The chaplain remained on board with those who stayed to work the buckets.

The boat remained on the beach all night, which was one of great danger for those still on board the *Atalaya*. In the morning some of those on shore returned to the ship to get food, which was not to be obtained on shore. The first boat arrived safely with the help of the surf-line, which helped to steady the vessel when the crew held on to it going through the breakers. But when the boat was returning for the second time it was overloaded because too many people from the ship crowded in in spite of the efforts of those on board to prevent them. The wind also freshened and the sea increased. Then, when the boat was some distance from the *Atalaya*, a Chinese on board cut the ship end of the surf-line with a hatchet (for reasons which Feyo does not give). The result was that when the boat reached the breakers there was no line to steady it. It broached and was swamped, and of the seventy souls in it fifty were drowned without those on shore being able to help them.

The boat was dragged ashore, where it arrived "all shattered". Feyo comments "And the sea cast up nothing of the many things which were embarked in it." He continues, "On Friday the captain gave orders to repair the boat, and offered five hundred xerafins (a silver coin used in Portuguese India before the nineteenth century) to any one who would go back in it to the ship to land those who were left; but no one would venture, the waves being very great and the fear inspired by the event of the day before still greater. Those on board afforded a piteous spectacle by their shrieks and cries to heaven, which though they were far off were such as to inspire great grief in those who were on shore. As there was now no refuge in the ship except abaft the mainmast, all the rest being under water, and all hope of the boat was gone, many threw themselves overboard on pieces of wood, and some reached the shore and others perished. The night before they fired a gun for us to assist them.

"The following night between Friday and Saturday some of our negroes came ashore and said that there were still white men in the ship, with no refuge but a rail of the poop on which was an image of our Lady of Atalaya; but at daybreak the ship went entirely to pieces, so that only a small hatch came ashore whole, and all the rest was in scattered timber. The sea cast up some of the chests which were on deck, but they were in pieces. To this was the wealth of such a mighty ship reduced, and here many found themselves poor and naked, who a short time before were rich and well clothed.

"The captain mustered those who remained, and divided them into three squadrons, taking the passengers for himself and dividing the seamen and ship boys among the officers. He issued an order that all provisions should be brought into the camp and put together, and appointed several men to go along the shore for the purpose, forbidding the others to leave the camp, which we removed into the bush, because on the shore where we landed we were covered with sand. We made shelters as good as canvas tents, in which we lodged, preparing ourselves for our anticipated journey through Kaffraria to Cape Correntes. All the provision found was placed in the camp and guarded. During the eleven days we remained there we suffered greatly from hunger and thirst, because of our lack of provisions and because the water had to be carried from the Infante river, a distance of nearly a league, and it was so bad that many fell sick through it. . . .

"On the eighth of July Dom Duarte Lobo went with the under-pilot Balthazar Rodrigues, Urbano Fialho Ferreira, of the order of Christ, son of Antonio Fialho Ferreira, and others, to the river Infante to measure the altitude of the sun, and they found the latitude 33°. The point of a ridge lying to the north-west was thickly wooded, the shore was more than two leagues in length, the coast was bordered with hills of white sand with trees on the top, and the mountain was bare. When they had measured the altitude of the sun an alarm was given that there were Kaffirs on the shore, and signs were made to them to wait. When they approached to speak no one could understand them, because they spoke with clicks. They go naked, and wear only a few skins. They sow no grain, and live only on roots, the produce of the chase, and some shell-fish when they come down to the shore. Their arms are of fire-hardened wood and a few iron assagais.

"When Dom Duarte Lobo and the others returned to the camp, the arms, balls, powder, a few cocoa nuts, the copper required for barter, and the lines and hooks for crossing rivers, were all divided and registered in the king's book. The rice was found to be all musty and rotten, and therefore we hastened our departure the more, burying the copper and powder which were left over.

"During the days we remained there the captain consulted with the pilot Gaspar Rodrigues Coelho, the notary Francisco Cabrita Freyre, and other sick persons who could not travel on foot, whether he should order the boat to be prepared for them and give them men to manage it, but the pilot would not accept the offer, and there was no further question about it, though it was the best plan to save these people and the women and sick from perishing, as will be seen hereafter. . . .

"More time was necessary to rest from our past labours and gather strength for what was in store for us, but our lack of provisions and the unhealthiness of the site obliged us to set out on Monday the 15th of July, in the morning, after we had all recited the litany of our Lady. It is impossible to state in a few words with what sorrow and tears this pitiful tragedy was begun, for we left there, because of the wounds with which they came ashore, a Kaffir belonging to the boatswain Manuel de Sousa, a little cabra* of mine, and a little negress belonging to the gunner Francisco Teixeira, who was drowned in coming ashore in the boat."

*The accepted meaning of *cabra* is she-goat; here it is used colloquially for an attendant of mixed blood.

Chapter 3

Both the *Sacramento* and *Atalaya* were huge ships for their time. The *Sacramento* was built at Bassein on the coast twenty miles north of Bombay by Rui dias da Cunha, Captain of Bassein, who won the commission for the ship from the Governor, Telles de Menezese. Her keel was laid in 1636. She was built to upper deck level and then towed to the river Panelim south of the main port of Goa for fitting out in April 1640 – Dutch reports show that she had slipped out of Bassein only three days before their blockading fleet arrived.

According to Portuguese records *Sacramento* was to be an unusually well armed ship mounting thirty guns a side (some, as the salvors discovered, Bocarro cannon) which would almost qualify her even two hundred years later as a major ship of the line. It is tempting to accept from this that she had been built specifically with the shipment of cannon in mind. According to Batavian marine records, however, the Dutch believed that the galleon was to be, not a sixty gun ship, but one of eighty guns, which would make her even more formidable if ever she broke out into the Indian Ocean. The information in the register was based on the reports of Dutch spies, probably misled by carefully planted Portuguese misinformation.

The Dutch were however correct in reporting that the ship was "very leaky", for although she was beautifully finished and a fine sight to the layman, the *Sacramento* was by no means a well-found ship. In fact the Dutch intercepted a letter sent by the Acting Governor of Malacca in 1640 in which he said that the galleon of da Cunha had arrived and was lying at anchor at Panelim. The ship had a heavy list as a result of a structural fault, concerning which he commented – "She is a beautiful piece of work but needs fixing and should be ready by next summer."

The Governor's estimate of the structural fault was dramatically understated. It took five more years' work before the *Sacramento* was ready to put to sea. In March 1643 the Dutch spies, in reporting that the vessel was going to mount eighty guns of bronze added "They are still busy working on it."

The great ship was still unfinished when the Dutch and Portuguese declared an uneasy truce in 1644 and a golden opportunity to sail her at once was missed. It was only in 1646 that she was moved to await the arrival of Ferreira's ships and the Bocarro cannon.

Lying almost alongside the *Sacramento* in the river was the *Atalaya*, built of pine in Portugal. She was an old but extremely big ship which brought the new Viceroy to India in 1640 and had thereafter been kept bottled up in the river by the blockading Dutch fleet. In the meantime, in March 1642, she had been newly sheathed with lead and made ready for sea; and with the truce in 1644 she took the first opportunity to sail. In December of that year her officers were hastily recruiting men for the voyage to Lisbon and she sailed eventually on December 29. She reached Lisbon on November 24, 1645, and sailed again for India in 1646, arriving in Goa in September.

It was in late January 1647 that the two ships were moved to await Ferreira's fleet. The Viceroy, Dom Filippe Mascarenhas, was entertained on board the *Sacramento* (which was to undertake her maiden voyage as the flagship of the two) by the Commodore, Luis de Miranda Henriques. He gave orders that once the guns had been transhipped the two ships, each of which also carried a general cargo of spices and a valuable casket of diamonds for the king, should sail as early in the same month as the weather would allow.

It was a colourful and moving occasion when the ships sailed, the more so because one of the ships was making her maiden voyage. It is not known that anyone on the *Sacramento* kept a diary; and if he did, it has not survived. But aboard the *Atalaya* a passenger, Bento Teyxeyra Feyo, kept a vivid account. It was dedicated to King John and published in Lisbon in 1650. It has been reproduced in full by the Cape historian George McCall Theal who used an eighteenth century counterfeit. Boxer says that no one has seen the original in recent years and that its whereabouts are unknown. Records in Lisbon show that there is a two-page difference in pagination between the 1650 publication and the eighteenth century counterfeit, but it is unlikely that this has made any significant difference to the account.

Feyo describes the scene, with small boats running in alongside the galleons to take off friends and relatives making their last farewells. At best they would not be reunited for two years, although the probability was that they would never see one another again. "The Viceroy came on board and gave orders to weigh anchor one morning as soon as the weather permitted. The officers preparing all things necessary and causing the sails to be loosened, the flagship first unfurled her foresail and spritsail, then the other did the same. There were on board many boats full of friends and relations, whose regrets increased the grief for which the taking leave for so long a voyage was sufficient cause; and thus with many heartfelt tears and wishes for a prosperous voyage we set out with the land breeze, which lasted three hours. Then a slight breeze arose and we kept along the coast . . ."

Aboard both ships were experienced seamen who feared that waiting in Goa for Ferreira would mean a long and hard passage down the south-east African coast in the winter gales.* To those aboard the elderly *Atalaya* the prospect of making a winter passage was particularly daunting as the old ship creaked and groaned her complaints. Feyo noted these fears early in his diary when the Commodore ordered the ships to investigate a passing merchantman. She turned out to be a friendly vessel bound for India, but for some reason not made clear the Commodore wanted to set fire to her. For four days the three ships lay together drifting while officers tried to persuade Commodore Henriques to let the ship go; which he eventually did. Feyo wrote: "Thereupon we left her on Tuesday March 5th. Men experienced in seafaring were of the opinion that the days we remained there without sailing would be disastrous to our voyage, and so we afterwards found, in the lack of favourable weather for reaching and passing the Cape of Good Hope." Later, in a flamboyant gesture, the *Atalaya* fired a seven gun salute to the Commodore on Easter Day – and the ship sprang a series of leaks along her waterline as a consequence. "This caused great anxiety to those who understood the danger to which we were exposed, because the ship was old and we were to attempt to pass the Cape in the depth of winter, when the tempests are numerous and such as to give great trouble to new ships" Feyo comments.

The ships must have been making slow progress from the point where they left the India-bound merchantman on March 5, for near the equator they were overhauled by the *Saõ Pedro O*

*Two lengthy notes printed on the Admiralty chart give warning of the frequency of gales, and of the vagaries of the currents, along the coast between Cape Natal (Durban) and Algoa Bay. "The severity of the gales of the Cape of Good Hope and the adjacent coast to the eastward, and especially in the neighbourhood of the Agulhas Bank" the chart states "is well known to navigators, as also is the rapidity with which they succeed one another, and their violence during the winter months (June to September)." It describes the Agulhas current as ". . . an enormous body of warm water which attains considerable velocity over the part between Cape Natal and Algoa Bay. During the winter months this current diminishes in force and extent, and the cold water setting from the higher latitudes repels and permeates it . . . The meeting of the cold and warm currents is frequently denoted by a broken, confused, and heaped sea; the warm current is also indicated by a marked change in colour of the water – this change of colour combined with the agitation of the sea frequently conveys the impression that the ship is in soundings" (near the shore where a hand-held lead-line would touch the bottom). This impression, a false one, would suggest the ship was off course when she was not.

Grande which had sailed from Goa on March 6. Feyo notes that the three ships continued in company for twenty days, until the *São Pedro* went ahead alone. It seemed so unlikely that the *São Pedro* was capable of such a turn of speed that it was at first assumed that Feyo was mistaken. But Boxer quotes a letter written on April 6, 1648 by Luis Botelio Frois, captain of the *São Pedro O Grande*, in which he recalls the meeting in "five degrees southern latitude". Frois says in the letter that he went on to the Cape, but was forced back to Mozambique when his crew became scared of the rough weather and mutinied.

Frois mentions that on his return to Lourenço Marques* from the Cape he heard that a "great dismasted ship" had been sighted, and said that he speculated at once that it must be the *Sacramento* or *Atalaya*. He finally rounded Cape Agulhas, "with the loss of many men" but he was forced to run for Brazil to carry out repairs; and in 1651 his ship was wrecked in the Azores. His speculation that the "great" ship must have been the *Sacramento* or *Atalaya* shows how big the two vessels were for the time; and while it is now impossible to say whether his guess was correct, the *Atalaya*'s main topmast had been carried away by June 10.

Parted from the *São Pedro*, the ships sailed on. Aboard *Atalaya* conditions were uncomfortable, not only because of the leaks caused by the gun salute, but also because the usual round of illnesses and deaths had begun. Feyo notes that the Inquisitor of India, Antonio de Faria Machado, who was returning home in the *Sacramento*, had died; and in *Atalaya*, "eight sailors, five artillerymen, four ship-boys, and some passengers".

If, as is likely, the pilot was using Perestrelo's chart, then by June 10 *Atalaya* was in latitude 33° south, somewhere on the Algoa Bay side of the Rio Iffante (renamed the Great Fish River and now marked by a lighthouse). The ship's maintopmast (the upper section of the mainmast) had broken; she was still leaking continuously, and the African slaves and ship's boys were at the pumps twice a day. Her captain, Antonio de Camara de Noronha, asked the *Sacramento* to stand by him for at least a week so that help would be at hand while repairs were carried out.

Then, on June 12, the storm broke which was to lead to the doom of both ships. "At nightfall the Commodore was in our company" writes Feyo, "and the breeze fell before sunset as we were sailing towards the land with the wind west-north-west. The sky grew very red, with heavy black clouds, and there was one flash of lightning, and we saw a fish orelhão (a type of jellyfish) a great portent, all signs of a tempestuous night. Then the wind began to blow harder, and we furled the topsails and spritsail, and the ship lay under her courses during the short watch and first watch. At the setting of the moon the sea rose, and the wind increased so much that the ship pitched and took in a quantity of water, and the yards and catheads (spars rigged on the mast to hold the sails) dipped into the sea. Order was given to haul down the mainyard, but through fear of the sea and such rough weather, and the inexperience of the artillerymen, they hauled in such a way that a gust of wind caught the sail, and the ship broached to (was forced beam on to the wind) in such a violent hurricane that it carried away the mainsail and foresail, tearing them to pieces with such an uproar that we thought the ship must founder."

It would appear from Feyo's account that the ship was now listing heavily with the weight of water she had taken in during pitching. This aggravated the situation when she broached by flowing to the lower side, thus forcing the ship even more on her side. From what he says later it also seems fair to assume that the cannon, weighing four tons apiece, also began to shift during this violent manoeuvre; for he writes that the ship lay broached to against the sea for a considerable time until they were able to get a stormsail set. With sail up the pilot (the term is Feyo's – we would say navigating officer) could then bring the ship into a safe course in relation to the following sea, and the water would drain away. If the cargo had shifted she would now

*Then the chief Portuguese settlement and port in Mozambique, named after a navigator commissioned to chart the area.

have a permanent, if slight, list. (The problem would have arisen whether the cargo shifted or not, for there was by now no sail set and the vessel would have little or no steerage way, but with her high fore and aft castles one would have expected her to come stern on to the sea fairly quickly; and with the wind driving against the aft castle the pilot would expect to broach as the ship surfed on succeeding waves.)

During the night the *Atalaya* was separated from the *Sacramento*, which while under great stress was probably making better going of the storm. By morning the *Atalaya* was a shambles. Her rigging was tangled, much of it was swept away,and she was taking in water. But the storm abated sufficiently for the crew to rig some small sails and cut away the wreckage of the rigging; and for several days, though she was badly damaged and the pumps had to be manned continuously, *Atalaya* continued to remain seaworthy. Her captain, realising that she had been swept out to sea, turned towards land in the hope of finding a lee shore to carry out temporary repairs. He hoped it might then be possible to turn back to Mozambique, winter there, and make more permanent repairs to his ship. Also in the captain's mind was his cargo of cannon for the king; and Feyo lends credibility to the idea that some of the guns had broken loose during the height of the gale by noting that Captain de Noronha wanted to "secure" the king's property and artillery if he made Mozambique. But he was overruled by the merchants aboard who according to Feyo "intimidated" the captain to continue, despite the damage to the ship, because they wanted to get their cargo to Lisbon.

After some days' sailing the *Atalaya* made landfall "in 32 degrees" (that is one degree further north than they were on June 10, having been blown back in the storm). This would have been about twenty-seven nautical miles north of the Rio Iffante. Perestrelo the cartographer had cause to remember the spot well, because it was here that the ship *Saint Benedict*, in which he was a passenger, ran on to the rocks and sank. In his description of it he said "The river Iffante is in latitude 32 degrees and a half. Its mark of recognition is its being high and rocky in the interior, with both its banks steep."

His better judgment overriden by the wishes of his merchant passengers and officers, Captain de Noronha continued sailing south towards Algoa Bay with passengers and crew manning the pumps night and day, "without exception, even to the religious (priests)" and making buckets from barrels to supplement the hard-pressed pumps. Here again Feyo noted the sloppy way in which the cargo was stowed. They had hoped to use the hatchways as "wells" through which to pass the buckets as they bailed, but found that this was not practical because ". . . the stowage of the artillery which was made in Goa not being properly done, leaving four guns in the hatchway".

From what followed it appears that the captain had by this time virtually lost control, for having gone below with some of his officers to inspect the ship he emerged on deck and ". . . with three nails from the lining in his hand, announced that the ship was fit to go to Jerusalem". Considering that she had been leaking from bow to sternpost since the gun salute, and that he had found some of the nails which should have held her together on his inspection below decks, it is likely that Captain de Noronha was speaking ironically, and that the ship was fit only to go to heaven. Later, when the weather moderated, he refused to order any repairs to the ship. He seems to have realised that she had hardly a hope of making the long voyage to Lisbon. A ship of her size, making water, would have had little response to her helm, and must have been almost impossible to control.

While the party from the *Atalaya* were taking stock of their situation on shore the *Sacramento* was still at sea fighting the storm. Although it was not until much later, when the survivors joined his party, that Feyo heard the story of the wrecking of the *Sacramento*, it is best dealt with at this point.

Feyo describes how he encountered the survivors from the *Sacramento* towards the end of November in the following words.

"When exploring a plain we caught sight of some people with hats, who with one on the end of a lance came forward shouting. The captain Antonio Carvalho, with others, went forward to meet them, thinking that they were strangers from the wreck of a boat which we had found broken on the shore. He found that they were from the wreck of the galleon *Sacramento*, our flag ship, and with great grief he returned with these shipwrecked sailors in his company, who were only five Portuguese, one Canarin, a mulatto, a Malabar, and a Kaffir, whom we all embraced with many tears, as men who met in a savage land so far from our country, and through so sad a cause as the loss of such ships with so many men and so great riches. We saw here nine persons who, unarmed, had travelled so far among so many barbarians, who laid an ambush every hour, from which God delivered them. Of their comrades who escaped from the wreck some fell by the hands of the Kaffirs, others died of hunger and hardship, and some remained behind alive because they had no strength to proceed. These nine were Manuel Luis, ropemaker of the galleon, whom they elected captain, Marcos Peres Jacome the under-pilot, the caulker, two Portuguese ship's boys, a mulatto, a Canarin, and two slaves."

The survivors said that after the storm which "overtook the galleon and the ship *Atalaya* . . . the galleon was left without a mainsail . . . With the stormsail close to the wind they steered east-north-east with the lantern alight, with great difficulty, springing many leaks, which were stopped after the storm was over, and they had done all that is considered effectual on such occasions. At daybreak," Feyo continues, "finding themselves separated from the ship *Atalaya*, running before the waves, which were very high, they turned towards the land, and were overtaken by another storm on the feast of Saint John. When it was over they pursued their course towards the Cape of Good Hope, without losing sight of the land after they had seen it. Sailing with the foresail set, very close to the shore, on the feast of Saint Peter, in the afternoon of the 29th of June, the waves being high, the chief pilot was directed to stand out to sea. This he did during one glass before sunset, pursuing that course for six glasses of the dog watch and eight of the first watch, and when the middle watch began, he steered for the land with the foresail set; and after six glasses the moon appeared and those of the watch announced that land was very close. On hearing this the pilot gave orders to stand out to sea, as the wind was gentle and the current setting strongly towards the shore.

"The galleon misstayed and would not turn completely about, in spite of the efforts which were made by unfurling the fore-topsail and sprit-sail. Her bow always turned to the shore, and she drifted towards it for two hours, in spite of the rudder and management of the sails, until rising on a great wave she struck from stem to stern and quickly went to pieces. The two galleries fell into the sea with the poop, and the chief captain Luis de Miranda Henriques, Father Sebastião da Maya, of the Company of Jesus, and many others, who after they came on deck, seeing there was no further hope, withdrew to the galleries to confess themselves; and only one of them escaped. Of the others, who had remained in the prow, some got ashore clinging to the yards, and some to pieces of timber, when it was clear daylight, amid great waves and reefs, to the number of seventy-two living souls, in latitude 34°.

The account which Feyo gives of the survivors' journey from leaving their landfall in latitude 34° until meeting the party from the *Atalaya* is short; but since they followed the track of those from the *Atalaya*, and that track has not yet been described, the journey of the *Sacramento* survivors will be more easily understood if it follows that of the earlier survivors.

Both parties of survivors, though at least a hundred miles apart by the shortest land route, determined to walk northward to Mozambique, a long march pock-marked by dozens of rivers some bigger than others, and some cut through deep and almost sheer cliffs. The journey is one of 800 miles, and was a remarkable undertaking. To have gone south to the Cape would have entailed a march of only 600 miles, but there was no settlement there and any ships in the bay could be expected to be unfriendly Dutchmen, whereas those in Lourenço Marques would certainly be Portuguese. It was also standard procedure to march close by the shore to Mozambique after being shipwrecked on the south-east African coast, and among the survivors were some who had done it before. There is no detailed account of what happened to the *Sacramento* survivors until the final stage of the journey when they joined parties, but it was such a remarkable undertaking that Feyo's description of his march with the *Atalaya* may be studied in its place.

As we have already seen from Feyo's account, the *Atalaya* party spent eleven days in camp while they collected along the beach everything useful washed ashore from the wreck, concentrating on goods which could be bartered with the Africans in exchange for guidance and food. The captain divided the party into three, keeping the passengers in his group, and splitting the seamen and boys among the officers. They determined to move when the party sent to shoot the sun at the Great Fish river told on their return how a party of Africans, "speaking in clicks" (no doubt a form of Xhosa dialogue) and armed with "fire-hardened wood and a few iron assagais" approached them in hostile manner. The arms, musket balls, cocoa nuts and copper which were to be bartered were shared among the parties, as were lines and hooks (presumably grappling hooks) for crossing rivers. The division of goods was punctiliously noted in the king's book. Several people, including the pilot Gaspar Rodrigues, elected to remain behind, either because they were badly wounded or too ill to contemplate the journey. They refused the captain's offer to supply them with men to man the ship's boat so that they could at least attempt an escape to safety, and the party prepared to move on.

Even in these extraordinary adverse circumstances the hard-headed commercial values and authority of class persisted. The noblemen and wealthy merchants among the survivors were able to buy what comforts were to be had by offering the seamen and slaves money, valuables and future favours in return for being relieved of manual work themselves. In those times the only safe way of conveying riches from the East to Portugal was in the form of gold or jewellery, and it was therefore the custom for the wealthy abandoning ship to swathe themselves in chains of gold and jewellery of all sorts. A very rich man would be encumbered with a great many heavy gold chains, and was more likely to be drowned through his own greed than by accident of nature. Feyo highlights all this in a telling paragraph: "Dom Sebastião Lobo da Silveira was so unfit for walking, being very much burdened with flesh and having other complaints, that he could not take a few steps on his feet; and therefore he asked the ship-boys, and the officers to persuade them, and it was arranged through the intervention of his brother Dom Duarte Lobo, who was beloved by all, that they should carry him in a net they made of fishing lines, he paying eight hundred xerafins to each ship-boy, to which Dom Duarte bound himself, giving pledges of gold. This nobleman was also sick, and in the camp we gave him up for dead; and he prepared a net with his negroes and two more whom he bought, and so attempted to accomplish the journey."

They set off on their long journey, the captain going first, the master Jacinto Antonio leading the van, and the boatswain the rear. Then, comments Feyo ". . . we began to feel the grief and misery of the sick and those incapable of keeping up with the company, judging from the beginning what it would be in the future. Beneath our eyes, when we had gone less than a league along the shore, Bartholomeu Pereira Loreta, a sailor, remained behind from fatigue, and the

Kaffirs who followed us immediately killed him, without our being able to assist him. Farther on the same Kaffirs took from Dona Barbara the wallet which she carried on her back with her share of copper and provisions and a diamond seal which had been saved, and if the rearguard had not hastened to assist her, they would have killed her as they did Loreto. As she could not keep up with us, Antonio Carvalho da Costa, a sailor, took her on his shoulders and carried her until nightfall. The Portuguese nun, Joanna do Espirito Santo, also gave great trouble, as well as the other sick. However we pitched our camp at last upon a ridge near the sea, where we found a spring of very good water; and the pilot, being unable to reach it, remained a gun-shot behind, and on his asking for confession the fathers attended to him with great charity and also to the notary, who waited behind and arrived very late at night. Here we passed the night.

"On Tuesday the 16th of July the captain called a council to determine what was to be done with the women and the incapable, who prevented us from travelling with the necessary speed to reach the land where we could barter provisions, for the few grains of rice with which we started from the place where we were wrecked amounted to so little that there was not more than two measures for each person, and according to the assertion of those who had already journeyed by that road we would find nothing to barter within less than a full month. After the matter had been well debated, seeing the state we were in and that the pilot, the notary, Dona Barbara, and Joanna do Espirito Santo could not accompany us, and by waiting for them we all exposed ourselves to perishing of hunger, it was resolved to tell the women to walk in front, there being now no question of the pilot and notary, for one was already speechless and the other past all hope, and that we would go forward the next day, leaving behind those who could not keep up with the company. When the Portuguese women were told this, they said they hoped God would go with us, but they dared not and could not. Therefore we left them after they had confessed themselves, together with a little negress who chose to stay with them; and they had no food whatever."

Dom Sebastião was also in danger of being left behind because the ship-boys who carried him found the work too hard and refused to do it; but Dom Duarte Lobo "with fair words and greater rewards" induced a few to continue. But the problem remained; and the ship-boys, because the road was bad and the food was little, decided to leave him. This they did; and he, fearing to go farther on foot, remained behind.

The captain and Dom Duarte had gone on ahead and did not immediately know that Dom Sebastião was missing. A group of sailors were persuaded to go back and fetch him. ". . . it being now night they went back two leagues and found him where he had been left. They brought him to the camp, which he reached very late, saying in a loud voice that Dom Sebastião Lobo da Silveira cared not for death, but for the bad treatment shewn to his person. The next day it was treated of with the sailors that they should carry this nobleman, from which task the ships-boys had desisted, the captain making many remarks upon his high rank and upon his having embarked for the kingdom on a summons from his Majesty.

The next day we advanced slowly, and almost within a league we came to the river of São Christovão. In order to cross it we made two rafts, the river being very full and deep, with a strong and violent current . . . Here Dom Sebastião confessed himself and made his will, giving up hope of being able to accompany us, and displaying many jewels and precious things of which no one knew, he offered them to any who would bear him on their shoulders. Seeing this, and upon the persuasions of the master Jacinto Antonio, to whom he gave six links of a chain of gold for the purpose, sixteen of the strongest sailors were treated with, to whom Dom Sebastião delivered all the things he had displayed."

That some members of the party were capable of taking a philosophical attitude to their fate is shown by the comment of one man left behind to certain death. He called to one of the friars "... and he, thinking it was some matter of reconciliation returned to hear what he wanted, and he said to him: 'Father Antonio, before you go do me the favour of a pinch of snuff, and may God be with you; and it would be a great consolation to me if they would dig a grave in this sand that I might get into it.'"

The saga of Dom Sebastião came to an end shortly after July 21 when the sailors found their health so impaired that they could no longer carry him. "And he, giving up hope resolved to remain behind, first of all set about confessing himself, and gave a ruby ring to each of those who had hitherto carried him, disposing of everything else, and even depriving himself of a metal cross with relics which he wore round his neck and a small copper kettle. He remained without any food whatever, for there was none, and all parted from him with just sorrow, leaving him under a little cloth tent, fat and in good health, with his strength unimpaired, because he would not venture to proceed on foot."

The story of the next few days' march is one of almost unbelievable hardship: of five days when the party had no food whatever; of one boy who came across a fire and took off his shoe, roasted it and devoured it greedily in order not to share it with anyone; of others who ate grass and risked death by eating poisonous wild beans. On one occasion members of the party going in search of shellfish found in a ravine a tiger's head, "very rotten, covered with vermin, and of an evil smell. They immediately ate the tongue and brought the rest to their master very joyfully. He set to cook it with his comrades and Dom Duarte Lobo, first drinking the broth and keeping such good watch that while it was cooking he stood ready with a gun to defend his prize from the others in case they should attempt to steal it ..." To such straits were the survivors of the *Atalaya* reduced.

Though the first part of the journey was a nightmare because of lack of food, the *Atalaya* party later came across Africans prepared to do barter. Each of the three groups of survivors therefore elected their own barterers, an arrangement which led to skullduggery and disorder on August 16, as Feyo recounts. "Here the Kaffirs came with cows, which we bartered from them. They were divided among the companies, some killing, some roasting and boiling, and all falling to with such a will that nothing was thrown away but the horns and hoofs of the cows, for all the rest was eaten. Other Kaffirs came down in haste with quantities of cattle, millet, and native bread, and there were some disorders among us, the barterers securing the most and best for themselves, scattering themselves in the thicket and waiting for the Kaffirs, from whom they bartered millet and native bread to the great prejudice of all, giving as much copper for a roll of native bread as was given in the camp for three or four.

"The Kaffirs, getting this price outside, brought down nothing but cows; and therefore a proclamation was issued forbidding any one to go and barter outside the camp under pain of death. But this did not suffice, for the hunger was not appeased even by the sight of so much meat. The master Jacinto Antonio was ordered to make rounds in the thicket and paths, to allow no barter, and to seize all those he might discover engaging in it. He found three Portuguese and three of our negroes, whom he seized and brought to the camp. A council was held, and the members thereof decreed that two of the three whites should be led through the camp by a rope, their offence being proclaimed, and their hands pierced; proof was wanting against the other. Lots were drawn to see which of the negroes should die, and it fell upon a mulatto belonging to Urbano Fialho, who was executed at once, and the two others were severely whipped through the camp."

Dom Sebastião's brother, Dom Duarte Lobo, apparently a man of stronger mettle, but equally incapacitated by good living in the past and with little ability to cope with his present circumstances, carried on bravely for some time until, on August 25 he was seized with an attack of flatulence which caused him great pain. "We assisted him with civet (made from the civet cat), a remedy which he used, it being an old complaint, and he grew better" Feyo records. "But suddenly it attacked him in the throat, hardly giving him time to make a fervent act of the love of God, at the last words of which his speech failed him, and he held in his hands a picture of Christ on the Cross. The father Friar Antonio de São Guilherme, seeing him in this state, called loudly on him to press his hand if he wished for confession, and he pressed it hard; then without further speech the father absolved him, and he immediately expired."

Dom Duarte Lobo's links with the *Sacramento* and with the increased production of iron cannon at Macao are interesting, for he had travelled to India with the Count de Linhares in 1629 when the latter had been appointed Viceroy and he, Dom Duarte, had been made commander of the fortress of Bassein (Bacaim in Feyo's spelling). His friendship with Linhares was lasting, and as a professional soldier he must have been keenly interested in the Count's efforts to increase Bocarro's output by ordering more iron, and fewer bronze, cannon. He commanded the fortress of Bassein until 1632 after having served in the State of India as soldier, captain, Chief Captain of the Fleets, and finally Governor of the Straits of Ormuz and the Red Sea. His links with Bassein, and the navy, would have inspired in him a great deal of interest in the building of the *Sacramento*. Feyo notes "He was on his way to the kingdom . . . rather to visit his Majesty than to seek a reward for all his services."

As the group moved on tensions grew, not only because of fights over the division of food, but also because some thought that the captain, De Noronha, was too weak a soul to lead men under such adversity. Thus Feyo, describing how on August 28 they went inland and camped in a level place near a river of brackish water, added "We remained a day in this place because of a revolt in the camp, some wishing to separate and saying that we ought not to travel all together, for there would not be enough barter for all. Thereupon the captain called a council, and all being dissatisfied because of his good nature, a separation was voted, but it came to nothing, because they could not agree upon the choice of a new captain and the division of the copper."

On August 30, however, the sailors and ship-boys again began to clamour that they wished to travel separately with the master, and that men, cattle, copper and arms should be divided. "To this the captain, lacking friends and advice, consented, first entering in the king's book the reasons and manner of this division, and how it was for the general good, because in some places there was a lack of barter and it was not sufficient for all, so that travelling in separate companies would be better. A division was made of the men, arms, cattle, lines, grapnels, kettles, and everything else." The company therefore set out in two groups, the captain's setting out two or three hours after that led by the master, of which company Feyo was a member.

On September 5 the members of Feyo's party bought cows, milk and native bread in plenty "in the midst of many kraals". But the day after they were led by two Kaffirs, who offered to guide them, into an open plain where they were "surrounded by Kaffirs as thick as starlings on the wing, uttering war cries and brandishing assagais, an infinite number to each of the Portuguese. But we, firing at them, though with little effect because of the distance, made them retreat, and they left us to pursue our way, still remaining in sight until we entered a wood thinking to get out of the way of these wretches.

"We ordered our march very carefully" Feyo continues "with armed men in the van and rear, the cattle in the middle, and a watch at each side, for the road was bad and very long and the Kaffirs lost no opportunity of molesting us, attacking us in the middle of the wood with loud shouts. But God helping us we immediately killed three, and without any damage on our side got out of the thicket near a spring of clear water. Here they brought us some provisions to barter, at which let no one who reads be amazed, for these people at the sight of copper will not heed though their fathers, mothers, and relations be slain."

In their further passage Feyo's group saw a large troop of lions "which went roaring through a valley without taking notice of us as we passed upon a height". They later forded a river which they called the Rio da Cruz because of a wooden cross they set up there, and because of another cross which they cut in a stone to let the other company know they had passed that way.

On September 12 the captain's company appeared; and they decided to travel as one company again, largely in order that they might defend themselves more effectively against the natives.

Not all the Africans were however unfriendly, for it appears from Feyo's report of the progress of the captain's party during the period of separation, that while there were marauding parties of small groups which would attack on any pretext, bigger groups living in orderly villages with cattle and crops were prepared to be hospitable in exchange for the highly prized copper they would receive. (Feyo does, however, report that one good-looking Kaffir they encountered, who was wearing many copper bracelets, said in Portuguese that he did not want copper for his cows but "silver like the moon and gold like the sun".)

A second attempt to divide the company was made by those sailors of the master's party who had the bulk of the copper for bartering; and this almost led to fighting. But the father Friar João da Encarnação flung himself in front of the guns levelled by one of the parties; and in the words of Feyo "upon his knees with a picture of our Lady of the Rosary in his hands, entreated them by that Lady and by the wounds of Christ to be at peace."

Thus everything passed off without offence, and at last all agreed that it was better for the safety of all that they should not divide. "Upon this" Feyo continues "the camp was formed again, and that day was spent in holding a council in which laws were propounded together with other matters conducive to good government, of which those were adopted which were approved by the vote of the father Antonio de São Guilherme, without whom nothing good could be done. Everything was entered in the king's books, which we all signed, companies and captains being appointed as before, and at nightfall we were in peace and contentment, thanking God who had delivered us from this evident peril."

On one occasion the company passed through a group of natives who received them with rejoicing, songs and dances. "We made our camp" says Feyo "in sight of them and of many kraals on a plain near a river, where they brought us such quantities of provisions to barter that there were more than a thousand loaves of crushed millet, the best bread in all Kaffraria, hens, millet, cows, goats, and sugar canes, all in great quantities . . . We spent nine days resting in this place and availing ourselves of the opportunity for bartering food, which was brought to us every day."

Feyo gives a delightful insight into the missionary zeal of the priests when he describes how on October 14 Father Francisco Pereira, finding an African called Alexander whom he thought to be wholly trustworthy and a man of God, declared his intention to remain, and go with the man to his village where he could convert the inhabitants to Christianity. The incident, like so many recounted by Feyo, is best described in his own words. "He spoke" says Feyo, "of this intention to the captain and other friends, who endeavoured to dissuade him with arguments which he would not admit, replying that it was nothing that he should give his life for the salvation of these souls, God having bestowed it upon him so many times when he was in danger in the midst of the misery on land and perils at sea through which he had passed in our company. With a smile on his lips and tears in the eyes of those who looked on, he gave away certain things, reserving for himself only an image of Christ our Lord and a metal picture of the

Nativity which he wore. Then he took leave of the company with great resolution, writing to the Archbishop Primate of India and to the viceroy to inform them of his intention.

"Taking with him the Kaffir Alexander and his son very joyfully, to whom a copper chain and other such trinkets were given, that they might be well disposed to the father, he set out for their kraal, leaving us in admiration. But as this design of the father was directed to the service of God our Lord, it was frustrated by the devil, for he found himself in the middle of the thicket abandoned by the Kaffir who guided him, and at a great distance from the place where we left him and where we were. He was obliged to return to the camp, grieved and disconsolate, with the image and picture which he took with him, and it was esteemed a miraculous favour from heaven that the Kaffir should have left them to him, and had not killed him to rob him, considering the esteem in which copper is held by these natives."

Towards the end of October the captain, confessing that his strength was not sufficient for the task, resigned his authority and Antonio Carvalho, a sailor who had already travelled through the land of Kaffraria, was elected as leader. He proved unpopular and the captain later resumed command.

By November 17 they had crossed the St Lucia river, the northern border of what is now Natal, and were in Mozambique. From this point Feyo and the party appeared to improve in spirits enormously, realising that they had come well over three-quarters of the distance and were within reach of Lourenço Marques. He records that they crossed a river believed to be one arm of the "river of the Golden Downs" and now known as the Kosi River.

Some time after November 22 – Feyo does not give the actual date – the *Atalaya* survivors met those from the *Sacramento*, who being far fewer in number had made faster work of the march. Their meeting has already been described, as has the wreck of the *Sacramento* reported by the survivors; it is now necessary to give the account of the journey northwards of those survivors as recorded by Feyo.

After they had landed the *Sacramento* survivors remained there eleven days without seeing a living being, refreshing themselves with such things as the sea cast ashore, which were very little. According to Feyo they then "journeyed onwards for a month before they found indications of the wreck of the *Atalaya*, and at the place where it occurred they found a little Kaffir girl and two little cabras who were maimed, from whom they learned the fate of the ship and that it was twenty-eight days since the people had left the place.

"There they provided themselves with powder and ball, of which they stood in need, and ate some leather which they found. Then they set out again and marched until they came upon Dona Barbara, whom they found alive near the nun Joanna do Espirito Santo, the pilot, and the notary, who lay dead. She grieved them enough by asking them to take her with them, and when they asked if she could walk she said no, and so they left her.

"They went forward until they reached the river where the ship *Belem* was lost (this is now the Belem River), where only ten of them arrived, some of the others having been left dead, killed by the Kaffirs or by famine, and some having remained behind alive because they could not walk. They were brought to such extremity of famine and misery that not a shoe or anything of the

---

Bringing the guns aboard. Clockwise from top left: A heavy gun comes out of the water lifted on the *Etosha's* special heavy lift gear. On the deck old car tyres have been laid to protect the wooden deck against the cannon rolling during the voyage to Port Elizabeth. (TR) One of the badly corroded cannon is lowered into the trawler's hold. Note the colour of the gun which would soon change to green as it oxidised; (LR) A heavy naval gun is hoisted inboard to be laid out on the tyres. The gun is covered in a crustacean known locally as red bait; (LL) A badly corroded gun hangs as the crew prepare to heave it inboard. The work was dangerous and hard, but throughout the operation it was conducted without mishap.

kind but was devoured even to a mariner's chart, which killed all those who ate it because of the mercury in the colours. They came to fighting hand to hand for a locust, which may well be imagined, for there was a day when five or six died of sheer hunger.

"From the river of the ship *Belem* onwards, though few and suffering great alarms from the barbarians every hour, they always followed the track of the people of the *Atalaya*, finding signs of it now and then, and getting information from the Kaffirs themselves, from whom God delivered them so far and allowed us all to meet again."

The next day the survivors from the *Atalaya* and *Sacramento* all journeyed together to the Kosi river, or the river of the Golden Downs as Feyo called it. All marvelled at its great width, the land on the other side being hardly visible because they were separated from it by more than three leagues of water. (In this case, since a Portuguese sea league was equal to four Italian miles of 1,480 metres, the river was some eleven miles wide.) They were shown the ford by two Kaffirs. "We entered it with great difficulty" records Feyo "the Kaffirs leading, with the water to our breasts. The day was cold, with wind, and a swell, and we crossed with the baggage on our heads and the cattle in the middle, and the water became more shallow, being below the waist. When we got near the shore on the other side there was another channel, where the water was up to our necks. We reached the other side towards three in the afternoon, wet and worn-out, as may well be imagined. We thanked God for his mercy in allowing us to meet with these Kaffirs, without whom it would have been impossible to attempt this ford, it being as wide as the sea of Lisbon near Barreiro."

Having crossed the river they found themselves in much improved circumstances, with gourds, water-melons, bolangas, tobacco available for barter and, as they journeyed farther, sesame, hens, fish, salt, millet, honey, butter, eggs, she-goats and sheep, all in such abundance that it seemed to the travellers that they had reached a land of plenty.

On December 14 they reached the court of King Unyaca and lodged in huts for the first time. They were told that a vessel from Mozambique had reached the island of Shefina twelve leagues away, and a party was sent to investigate. They there found a galliot (a small swift galley moved by sails and oars), and were hospitably received by the crew. "The captain Diogo Velho da Fonseca, a native of the town Villa Franca de Xira, married and settled in Mozambique, had gone to found the factories (trading stations) of Manisa, Manuel Bombo, and Locodone" writes Feyo.

"Being advised there of our shipwreck and arrival at Unyaca, like a good vassal of his Majesty (whom may God guard) he immediately sent our people back with a Moorish pilot with cloth for the expenses of the journey and the small skiff and trading lusio in which to cross the rivers of Lebumbo and Machavane. Antonio Carvalho and his companions, on their return with such good news, were received by us with great rejoicing and demonstration of the pleasure we all experienced, especially when we knew that this was the only vessel which had come thither for four years, which we attributed to the goodness and mercy of God, may He ever be ever praised for His Divine Providence."

They left the kraal with a party of Africans with whom they had become friendly, and made all haste to the place where the galliot was. The end of their long journey may be given in Feyo's own words. On the last day they set out early in order to be in time to hear mass on arrival, and came in sight of the galliot at eight o'clock in the morning. "Great was our joy at the sight, and some could not believe their eyes when they thought of all the hardships, famine, thirst, cold, and heat which we had endured . . . on the 5th of January, the eve of Twelfth Night 1648, we set out at once for the church of straw which was built there . . . to render thanks to God and to the Virgin of the Rosary to whom the church is dedicated.

"The captain Diogo Velho de Fonseca with his comrades of the galliot came to the shore to receive us with great joy and affection. The next day he divided among us all enough rice and sesame for three days, and supplied many with linen and shoes, and those who afterwards availed themselves of his larder were provided with sweetmeats and all the dainties he had for the sick, and none were refused . . .

"On the third day after our arrival the people of the ship and galleon, numbering a hundred and twenty-four Portuguese and thirty negro slaves, were divided among the five factories already established twenty leagues up the river, where there was no lack of food, for which three pieces of cloth a month were paid for each person, on His Majesty's account. The captain remained on the island the guest of Captain Diogo Velho, and the religious, officers, and ship's passengers were accommodated in straw huts which were newly built and in others which the Lascars of the galliot were paid to vacate. We spent six months on this desert island, going nowhere but to the factories, to which some repaired for provisions and refreshment."

In spite of having survived the dangers and tribulations of shipwreck, and of the long journey through at times barren and hostile country, many died during the six months they spent at the island and trading stations from plague, fever, and an over-abundance of food.

"When the time came to depart," Feyo continues, "all the survivors assembled in the factories and embarked, weighing anchor on the 22nd of June in the afternoon, with the spring tides, steering among beacons, the bay being full of shoals. Having cast anchor at the island of Unyaca we bartered many hens and sweet potatoes, and setting sail on the feast of Saint John we steered out course for Mozambique, with three hundred persons, white and black, in the galliot, for the most part sick and ill accommodated, for the ship was small. On the 9th of July we cast anchor opposite the fortress . . . On reaching the port Captain Diogo Velho went ashore, and presently returned angry enough with the governor Alvaro de Sousa de Tavora, with orders that none should land nor any boat be suffered to approach us save that of the governor, in which we were all taken to the fortress, where with the auditor, factor, and his notaries, he held an enquiry both concerning the loss of the ships and of the diamonds which escaped. Thence each one withdrew to such place as he found convenient, until it was time to embark for India . . .

"On the 11th of September we set sail with the land breeze, five ships in all, three for Goa, the pinnace for Diu, and the other for the islands of Comoro . . .

"The galliot being small and a bad sailer, the captain yet managed so that in spite of calms, storms, and contrary winds, she alone reached Goa that monsoon, coming in sight of land after forty-seven days between Angediva and Cape da Rama. Land breezes and others failing us, and not knowing the state of Goa harbour, by the unanimous opinion of all we turned back and entered the harbour of Onor on the 1st of November, fifty-two days after we had left Mozambique. On the day following, the 2nd of November, I set out for Goa with the fathers in a boat of fourteen oars and arrived there on the 8th of November in the morning."

Feyo mentions that 1647 had been a disastrous year for shipwrecks in Goa and that among other losses was that of the urca of the governor of Mozambique "which contained the wealth and resources of that city and the diamonds which escaped from the ships."

It is fascinating that the survivors should have carried what was apparently a large amount of diamonds all the way to Mozambique while their very lives were at stake; but the possession of the diamonds by the captain tends to explain why his party temporarily broke away from the rest, presumably in the hope that the diamonds could be shared among them when they reached safety. It is Boxer's opinion that the governor's boat was probably pirated by the *Atalaya* survivors aboard it, including the captain de Noronha, and was sailed to some distant port.

Certainly nothing was ever heard of the captain or the diamonds again, while Feyo survived to bring his account of the wreckings to Lisbon.

Feyo ends his diary with the following words: "I am in doubt as what to marvel most, whether at the certainty with which disasters occur at sea, or the confidence with which navigators always expect to escape them. Foreign authors may say what they choose: the Portuguese nation alone in the world was born with the gift of discovering the secrets of the land and sea."

Chapter 4

The *Sacramento* ran aground at a point which we would today describe as being south-west of Port Elizabeth, and nine miles east of the lighthouse at Cape Recife. It was on an uninviting stretch of coast between Sardinia Bay to the east and the village of Schoenmakerskop (literally "shoemaker's head or cliff") to the west.

The Admiralty chart calls the area "foul ground". It is just that – vicious currents swirling in and out among the reefs which lie just offshore, and a succession of small, shallow bays which build up from Cape Recife to Schoenmakerskop into cliffs falling perhaps a hundred feet to the jagged rocks below. Farther along, and nearer the site of the wreck, the cliffs drop away rapidly so that it is not difficult to walk down to the shale beach.

The shale, which is uncommon on most South African beaches, is unpleasant to walk on barefoot because it is made up of sharp pieces of shell fragments. The coastline consists of high rocks inshore with many gullies running between them, with long reefs stretching in places yards out to sea. In some spots there are more reefs even farther out. Towards Sardinia Bay the coast becomes a little more friendly; and at Sardinia Bay itself, though the currents are treacherous, there is a long sweep of magnificent beach running away as far as the eye can see down the coast towards Cape Town.

The stretch between Sardinia Bay and Schoenmakerskop is one which few people frequent, though fishermen sometimes go there to try their luck in the gullies, and lone walkers keen to be by themselves for a good two or three miles can sometimes be seen. The beach is narrow, leading at once into sandy foothills covered with low thick gorse, much of which contains a skin irritant, and through which none but the most determined would wish to walk. Schoenmakerskop, at the top of cliffs, often blasted by gales of unusual ferocity blowing in from the sea, is an anachronistic little community which until the 1960's resisted modernisation in the form of street lighting. It is here that the elderly or those wishing to get away from the city find the isolation they enjoy, while being only ten minutes by car from the suburban areas of Walmer and then Port Elizabeth. The village has, however, become reluctantly well known in recent years, for it is here that South Africa's best known international playwright, Athol Fugard, lives. Fugard actually moved house once when others were built too close to his for comfort.

It was to Schoenmakerskop that his parents would take David Allen to play in the rock pools, or walk along the shore, often for hours on end. His father was a retired merchant seaman and naval commander, and any walk with him would be side-tracked into lengthy explorations into every gully and nook as David was instructed in the ways of the sea and its creatures. Each passing ship would be examined and criticised for any apparent error in navigation – passing too close to the shore, too far off, or steaming too fast in heavy seas. On occasions they would be diverted from Schoenmakerskop in to going farther afield, but inevitably they would return to their favourite isolated rocks which they came to know intimately.

An incident which took place before his father retired from the South African Naval Reserve perhaps sparked what became David's ever growing interest in that stretch of coast. As its contribution to International Geophysical Year the navy was asked to co-operate in laying underwater long range wave recording instruments which would help to measure wave action around the world. In Port Elizabeth the ideal scientific spot was just west of Schoenmakerskop, but it could not have been a more impractical location from a seaman's point of view even if it had been especially chosen with that in mind. The instruments were to be laid about a quarter of a mile offshore and kept down with cement weights. A rubber hose pipe containing a line carrying electrical impulses was to be run ashore across the rocks, into a gully, and back to the recording instruments on the protected rocks behind the main bulwark of rocks facing the sea.

The task was virtually impossible. There are only a limited number of days when any vessel, let alone the elderly seventy-two-foot wooden hulled harbour defence motor launch then based in Port Elizabeth, could approach the shore with any degree of safety. Usually the surge of the waves, backed by an almost constant offshore wind, made it madness to come inshore there. Yet the operation was attempted, using in turn divers, a rocket line, rubber dinghies, and in the end a volunteer diver who risked all to swim out in the gully and carry a line between the boat and shore. Through all the attempts – which went on for several weekends – David would stand ashore and watch as the launch surfed in dangerously near the rocks, at times carried right over the reefs before she could be sent astern with just sufficient water below the keel to take her clear. Perhaps the operation itself was madness, for once in place the instruments worked for about a fortnight before the rubber hose was severed by being continually rubbed against the sharp rocks; and as far as is known nothing of any major scientific importance was born of it.

Still, to those on the shore it had instilled an interest in the sea, and in particular in that piece of coast, which lasts to this day. And thereafter David became closely associated with the sea.

Algoa Bay, discovered by Bartholomew Dias on his initial voyage round the Cape, is tucked in between the rolling sand-dunes which stretch from the point of Cape Recife in the north-east to the tip of Cape Padrone in the north-west. When Perestrelo came to chart it he noted that it was "A great open unsheltered bay . . . it may have a mouth of ten or twelve leagues across". He named it the Bay of Wolves because of the large number of sea lions he saw, but later reluctantly agreed to accept the more generally used, but less exciting, name of Algoa Bay.

Once there was a river called the Baakens at the head of the bay, up which substantial ships could sail in the early nineteenth century. The cliffs on either side were a magnificent sight. They were grassed over, and the cliff faces covered in vegetation of all sorts; but with the development of the city of Port Elizabeth, which sprang up rapidly after the arrival of British settlers in 1820, that all disappeared. The Baakens today is relegated to a narrow open sewer with only an occasional flood to remind one of its mighty past. The city is the Detroit of South Africa, with the plants of Ford and General Motors and the dozens of auxiliary factories which tag themselves to car manufacturers, the biggest source of income and employment in the area. In all it is a somewhat forlorn place, windswept, the business area winding along the bottom of a steep hill where it developed historically, and with huge suburban areas spreading across the unrelieved boredom of the flats which stretch along the main road to Cape Town. As Dickens had it in *Hard Times* "There is nothing here which is not severely workful". Even the harbour lacks the excitement of most seaports. There is little fishing, so the colourful characters at the trawler jetty are kept to a handful; and the port itself, although growing now with the advent of containerisation, handles the most mundane of cargoes. Entertainment for the young is severely restricted, and many tend either to fall into a dull factory clerk routine, or to leave as soon as they can for Cape Town or Durban, or Johannesburg inland.

It is not surprising that David turned to the activity he knew so well and which was so easily available. At the age of fourteen he turned to the thrill of meeting the sea on her own terms, underwater. With nothing more than a snorkel and flippers he spent hours under the sea, qualifying himself a year later to join the Dolphin Underwater Club. For its size and limited funds this is a dynamic organisation which undertook to control diving in the area, though it had no legal and only persuasive powers. In particular it kept a watchful eye on anyone, like David, venturing into the water with a speargun. But spearfishing soon palled for him, though he continued to associate with the club members who found it the chief fun of diving. Instead he turned to underwater photography and concentrated on scuba diving, having by this time acquired an aqualung and a wet suit. (The name scuba comes from Self-Contained Underwater Breathing Apparatus.)

Slowly his interests grew ever further away from those of the majority of club members. He took up instead with the husband and wife diving team of Chris and Anne Rennie. Formerly married to best-selling novelist Wilbur Smith, Anne was particularly dynamic, and devoted to diving. She and David provided the trio with the enthusiasm while Chris, who did not lack enthusiasm himself, provided the solid safety backing, and that knowledge of the dangers of deep diving and how to overcome them which welded the team into a particularly good and close-knit one.

Together they determined to make exceptionally deep dives, which is dangerous when using the simple gear they had and with only compressed air and not a mixture of gases in their tanks. Over a depth of 120 feet it became really dangerous, and they went down only one foot more each weekend so that they could carefully monitor their reactions to sonic changes and the effects of vision channelling (at such depths the normal wide scope of sight narrows to a few degrees either side of straight-ahead). In the end they called it a day after diving to a depth of 200 feet, which was certainly a record in Port Elizabeth and perhaps for the whole coast. In 1971, having matriculated from the Grey High School, David joined the South African Navy as a national serviceman.

In 1972 he returned to Port Elizabeth to work for a tyre manufacturing company and continue his diving. He now also led a police reserve squad (with the rank of warrant officer) which was kept constantly busy recovering bodies, murder weapons and firearms; and gave diving lessons at the fledgling University of Port Elizabeth. Here he met Gerry van Niekerk, the stocky, powerfully built son of a sheep farmer from the Aberdeen district of the Eastern Province. They forged a lasting friendship almost at once. Gerry was exactly David's age and somewhat perplexed by his role as an accountancy student, so he tended to devote much of his time to diving.

David put him through the tests for the third class diploma in diving. Gerry's first aqualung dive was remarkable. David had decided that Gerry was unusually competent with a snorkel and above all never appeared to panic under the water. Together they went to the harbour, dived into the muddy waters and swam close together, the visibility being only a few feet. David led Gerry through his favourite spot, a hole in the solid breakwater in which he often found crayfish. Gerry, not realising where they were, went through the tricky hole in blissful ignorance – which changed to sharp consternation when he surfaced in the bay with the waves hammering up against the wall behind him.

The next dive was equally hair-raising, and little better for Gerry's nerves – a plunge to eighty feet in a water reservoir not far from Port Elizabeth. Gerry realised he had been thrown in at the deep end, and he enjoyed it! The competition excited him. Together he and David improved and refined their techniques, developing the sort of close teamwork which later allowed them almost to hold conversations underwater through gestures and mouthing of words. For a short time they were able to keep up with modern techniques at first hand because the Royal Navy frigates which called with some frequency at Port Elizabeth before 1974 (when the arms embargo slowed them to a trickle) would invariably have a diving officer keen to see the local underwater sights.

Gerry joined the police diving squad, and together he and David found themselves spending almost all their spare time in the sea on one pretext or another. In 1974 they carried their hobby to the perhaps slightly absurd lengths of breaking the world underwater endurance record by sitting in the Port Elizabeth musuem's oceanarium tank for twenty-four hours thirty-five minutes. They were helped in the dive by Lionel Harrison, who had established the first record of twenty-three hours some years previously in Durban. Both men were badly swollen and fatigued after using over a hundred air bottles and breathing twice the normal amount of compressed air; but they showed no long-term effects.

For some time their attention had begun to focus on the hundreds of wrecks which litter the coast. Some of these wrecks are historic; some date from the Second World War when German submarines had a field day on the long and unprotected coastline; and some are the consequence of inevitable modern marine accidents. As they turned their attention to salvage they realised there would be little interest in becoming "salvage" divers – underwater scrap metal merchants – as David calls them, simply diving to pull up metal for sale to dealers. They would rather enter the pioneer field of marine archaeology.

"I think we had the right disposition," comments David. "Neither of us are academics but we are able to do thorough research, and we had the enthusiasm and sense of the dramatic which kept us going on when at times the results were hardly gratifying."

The beginnings were humble. They found a well-known Dutch wreck in Sardinia Bay, the twenty-eight gun "korvet" *Zeepard* built in 1817 at the Admiralty yard in Amsterdam by P. Schuyt and wrecked in 1823. From it they salvaged some remarkable artefacts including muskets and grape shot – balls of shot in muslin bags with a wooden base, which when discharged tore the enemy's sails to shreds and sometimes also killed sailors clambering up the masts to alter the sail settings.

Later David and Gerry moved to the Cape and worked on the *Meerestyn*, a Dutch East Indiaman wrecked in Saldanha Bay in 1702, from which they recovered silver coins and various small artefacts including gold buttons. But team diving came to an abrupt but temporary end in 1976 when Gerry was obliged to return to the family farm to learn his father's business.

David resigned his job after a car accident in which he suffered indeterminate brain damage. This left him continually drowsy so that he would fall off to sleep even as he sat talking as a passenger in a car. Having satisfied himself as to the extent of the injury, and concluded with expert advice that it was in all probability permanent and irreversible, he realised that there was little point in moping in bed, but that he should drive himself to learn to live with the problem, and to carry on as he had done in the past. The obvious alternative was to continue diving; but this was dangerous without his old partner, and he ventured back gingerly, feeling his way. The accident did, however, provide time for research. This he did mainly in the Port Elizabeth Library, where the chief librarian, Alf Porter, a delightful man with a dour sense of humour, was only too happy to initiate him into the basic techniques of research. He had also made a close friend of the harbour engineer, the Hollander Hans Huisman, who was a prominent member of the local Historical Society and a board member of the museum.

David soon decided that the over-riding problems in historical salvage, at least in Port Elizabeth, were that the local divers tended to do more talking about how they intended to salvage treasure and make their fortunes than actual diving; and that each one claimed to have locked away "secret" information not available to anyone else. "I would spend hours in the Dolphin and Maritime club bars hearing how everyone knew where this or that wreck was, and how it was just a matter of going out next Saturday and hauling a fortune out of the sea with no effort at all," David said. "These fellows were all well meaning and without exception delightful chaps, but the fact remained that they seldom did go out to find that fortune, and I knew that as they had mostly dived around Port Elizabeth all their lives they would inevitably resent a

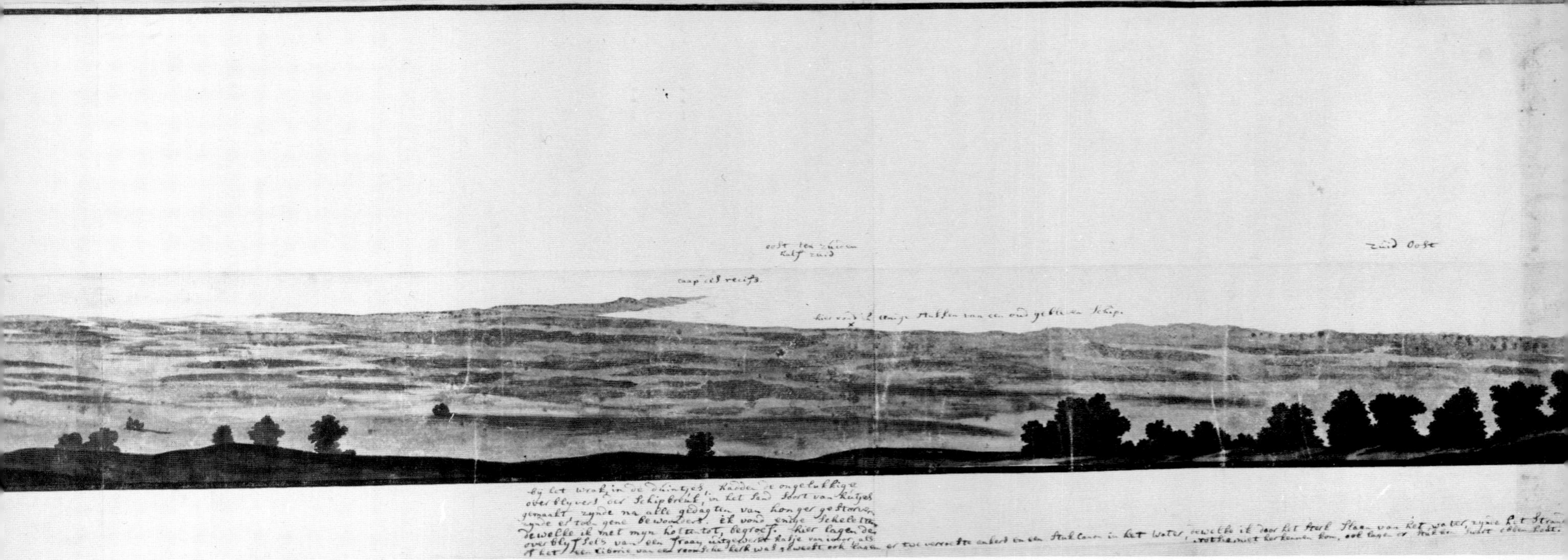

Gordon's map of the site of the *Sacramento* wreck. The cape in the centre is Cape Recife, while the "x" to the right of it marks the spot where Colonel Robert Gordon found the cannon and anchors which marked the site as well as the camp in which the survivors had lived ashore before making their incredible trek north.

The map was made in 1778 and is now housed in the Rijksmuseum in Amsterdam.

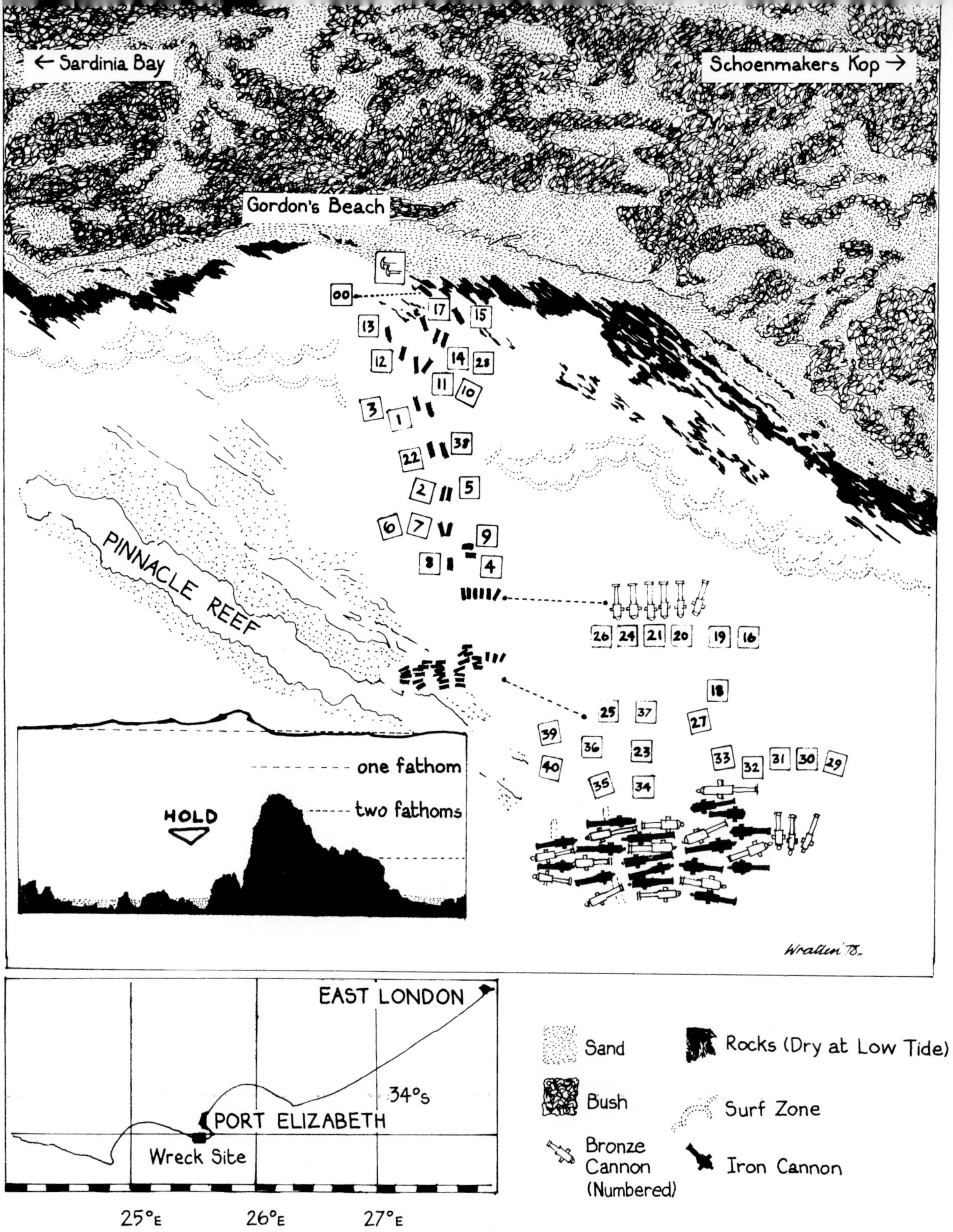

The site plan. The cannon marked "OO" is the one found and salvaged in 1951 by Mr. Hal Harraway, the others are those found by David Allen and Gerry van Niekerk. The iron cannon have been left on the site for fear that they would corrode as soon as they were lifted into the air. The bulk of the cannon were found in the ship's hold, bottom right on the plan, stacked on the ocean floor exactly as they had been in the ship's hold. The others were spread across the seabed as the bow and forecastle were carried inshore by the succeeding waves. Inset is an echo sounder profile of the reef which the *Sacramento* struck and which ripped out her hold. The profile shows that the divers were working in the surf in only three fathoms (18 feet) of water. The village of Schoenmakerskop is off to the right of the site.

smart-alec youngster such as myself, particularly if I found anything worthwhile." He concluded that while a certain degree of secrecy would be essential to a properly conducted salvage operation, the important thing was to gather and collate as much information about as many wrecks as possible, and to talk to anyone who would discuss the subject. Unlike most other divers, he did not intend to bet everything on one or two accounts of any particular wreck.

"From almost as far back as I can remember being interested in wrecks, the two which fascinated me, and which from time to time came up in newspaper features and other articles, were the *Sacramento*, and a British East Indiaman the *Dodington* which was reckoned to be a treasure ship," David said.

His research both ashore and at sea started in earnest in 1972, but by 1976 he felt he had both the time and an increased motive for pursuing the venture. His decision to keep an open mind and to piece together every different account paid off rapidly, for it did not take long in the library to discover that virtually every author on the subject put the *Sacramento* in a different position, almost all of them placing her somewhere near the *Atalaya*, and one as far up the coast as Mozambique. Clearly he would need to stick closely to original sources.

One morning he went to see Hans Huisman to discuss some historical aspect of the *Zeepard*; but this became lost as the conversation wandered to "Gordon's wreck". Both men had long been fascinated by the wreck found and mapped near Schoenmakerskop in 1778 by the extraordinary Colonel Robert Jacob Gordon, who was in the employ of the Dutch East India Company; and in Huisman's big office overlooking the busy harbour with its dusty red ore berth they speculated as to what ship it might be.

When David left the office he drove thoughtfully home and got out his photostat copy of Gordon's map with its marginal annotations. He had long believed that Professor Eric Axelson (who found the fragments of the original Dias cross which had been planted at Kwaai Hoek, charted now as False Island) was nearly correct when he put the *Sacramento* at Cape Recife. "There was no record of a wreck along there, and the bottom is so clean and sandy that unless it was completely buried it would have been found," David said. That night he pored over Gordon's map for hours.

Gordon was a Hollander of Scottish descent who became the commandant of the Dutch garrison at the Cape toward the end of the eighteenth century. He was a remarkable man in many respects, not least because he was able to smuggle merino sheep out of Spain against the strict orders of the authorities and establish what is today a multi-million-pound wool exporting business in South Africa. Eventually he committed suicide, but before that he spent years travelling through South Africa, sticking mainly to the coast and making maps and sketches as he went. On his map of 1778 he marked Cape Recife clearly; and well to the south east, almost exactly where Schoenmakerskop was later established, he pin-pointed a wreck (literally with the traditional "X" of all treasure maps) he found while walking on the beach. His marginal note in Dutch has been translated as: "Near the wreck, in the dunes, the remaining miserable castaways had built some shack shelters in the sand, now without habitants as everybody thinks they died from hunger. I found some skeletons which with the help of my Hottentot I buried. Here the remains of a beautifully carved little box chest of ivory were laying around, which might have been a shrine for a Roman Catholic chalice; also two rusty anchors and a cannon, which as the breakers were strong, the beach rocky, I could not recognise, also some pieces of ebony."

The site must have been remarkably preserved, for Gordon concluded that the wreck was comparatively recent. There is one point worth noting, and that is why Gordon should have gone down to the coast at precisely this point. It may be that it was because his companion on many travels, an artist J. Schumaker, wished to paint a seascape. Schumaker had previously painted the Van Stadens river to the east of Schoenmakerskop, and was later to do a painting of the Sundays river to the north-west of Port Elizabeth, so it would not be surprising if he wanted to paint a scene between the two. No such painting has survived, but the suggestion gives a possible derivation for the strange name of the area – Schoenmakers (Schumaker's?) kop (headland) – and would explain why his friend Gordon was strolling along the beach.

David became increasingly fascinated by Gordon's wreck. He felt certain the *Sacramento* was somewhere in that area, and discounted any theory which put it to the west of Cape Recife – for in that case why would the survivors have had to walk for a month before finding the miserable castaways of the *Atalaya*? Clearly, too, the bigger ship was more seaworthy according to Feyo's account, and had been blown out to sea rather than back along the coast like the *Atalaya*. He had little doubt therefore that the *Sacramento* too had entered Algoa Bay. Therefore she must be somewhere not too far beyond Cape Recife, but not close to the cape because there were no rocks there on which the ship could have struck in the dramatic fashion as described by Feyo.

Some time later David went through the documents in the museum library left by Mr H.G. "Hal" Harraway, an enthusiastic amateur historian. Harraway was told in 1951 of a cannon wedged in the rocks just beyond Schoenmakerskop. With great difficulty, operating from the shore and with a team of Africans, he recovered the gun and brought it to the museum. In September 1960, Harraway wrote to the Director of the Netherlands Historical Maritime Museum asking for help in establishing the background to the wreck of the *Zeepard*, earlier mentioned, and in identifying what he described as a twelve-foot 6,000 pound bronze cannon. He rightly pointed out that the wreck of the *Zeepard* lay about two miles to the south-east of the spot where he had found the cannon; and in fact David and Gerry later relocated her, as did members of the Dolphin Club, in Sardinia Bay. In his letter Harraway wrote, "According to the experts who have tried to decipher it the inscription should read, 'Conraet Wegt W oert me fecit Hagae.' " He said he felt the wreck was that of a Dutch East Indiaman. In fact because of the markings on the gun Harraway seemed determined to prove that the wreck was Dutch, and devoted much of his time to writing treatises on the subject.

David was intrigued. He felt certain that Harraway had found Gordon's wreck, but had made an incorrect deduction about its origins and failed to note Gordon's pointed reference to the Roman Catholic nature of the remains he found. As he pondered over Harraway's letter, David thought it entirely unlikely that a Dutch seaman or passenger would be a Roman Catholic; after all, differences over religion had been the basis of the Thirty Years' War.

David went out to inspect the cannon which Harraway had found, and looked at it carefully where it stood on its mounting outside the museum. He could find no trace of an inscription, so he went back inside to look at the photographs sent to Holland by Harraway. Again, if there was an inscription he certainly could not read it. Then he went on reading through the Harraway papers and came across the reply from the Netherlands Historical Maritime Musuem. Oddly enough it was dated June 9, 1964, apparently a full four years after Harraway's original letter seeking information. The letter read in part, "The inscription on the bronze gun should be 'Conraet Wegewaert me Fecit Hagae'. It is the name of a gunfounder working at the Hague during the middle of the 17th century until 1664, and maybe from 1616. So the wreck mentioned in the records of Colonel Robert Jacob Gordon was a ship from the 17th century."

David was elated. He was sure now that Gordon was wrong in assuming that the wreck was recent. Furthermore, on re-examining the position at home later, he realised that if Harraway's gun had come so far inshore it must have been a ship's gun mounted in the bows, and could therefore easily be Dutch, perhaps having been captured and mounted in the *Sacramento*. It was more likely, he thought, that the identification of the inscription was wishful thinking because nothing of it remained, although admittedly the gun had been sand-blasted in an effort to remove maritime accretions.

He and Gerry, who was now making trips from the farm as often as possible, were now becoming convinced that they had only to find Gordon's wreck to find the *Sacramento*. "Gerry and I had swum over the area every time the weather permitted, using snorkels because it is a waste of time and effort to use the more cumbersome aqualung for searching. You consume too much air to make it a proposition, as you always have to return to fill the bottles which only hold a half hour's supply. As we got more used to spotting things we developed a technique of towing one another behind an inflatable rubber boat powered by an outboard engine. This meant we could do four or five knots and cover a vast area of sea floor in a portion of the time it would take to swim it.

"When the weather was bad we used to walk along the beach, particularly at low tide. We were convinced, even though it was 300 years later, that if Gordon could see the anchors, so could we. On the balance of probabilities such big items do not simply disappear without a major hoo-hah being created. We were now sure that both Professor Axelson and Harraway had overlooked Gordon's find, and that there was a mis-identification in the case of the Harraway gun."

By late 1976 a complicating factor had arisen which increased their sense of urgency. Gerry was called-up to go to a periodical national service camp in the army and would have to leave at the end of January 1977. Until now things had been manageable, with Gerry making trips from the farm, but with the weather due to turn in late January they could lose a year's diving on the *Sacramento* site unless they found her now. Both believed that their work on the other minor wrecks – and the hours they had spent poring over drawings and sketches of ship's equipment and photographs of salvaged artefacts – had given them a major advantage in that they had a good idea what they were looking for.

Chapter 5

January 29, 1977, dawned a perfect summer morning as the men awoke at David's parents' home in Walmer. They loaded the diving gear into the boot of his car and drove out on to the Sardinia Bay road, driving past the race horses exercising at the course just visible from the road, and slowing down to turn on to the beach road. The tarmac sweeps round to the left between two sand dunes, and ends abruptly in a mound of sand rather like a crash barrier only 150 yards from the sea. They parked, got out to inspect the sea briefly, and dressed for the dive, delighted that the water looked clear and the weather seemed unlikely to change.

They backed through the surf in the typical manner of divers. Walking forwards means that one has to "fight" the broad edge of one's flippers into the waves, and put on face masks – the surf here is treacherous and it can take an hour to get into water fit for swimming.

The plan was to swim a hundred yards apart, and cover a mile of coastline parallel to the shore where the water was fifteen feet deep. They believed that this was a reasonable depth for the ship to have struck in, bearing in mind that most ships of the period were small and of shallow draught. Keyed up, they began what looked like being a long and exhaustive search. If the first sweep proved useless they would stop and plan another, perhaps slightly farther out, or more down the coast. Together they launched themselves forwards swimming at snorkel depth, moving slowly to ensure they missed nothing.

The water was clear except for some sand whipped off the bottom by the lazily rolling breakers. Suddenly David's attention was caught and held by the most fantastic sight he had seen underwater. In the sand below him was a perfect bronze cannon, its ten foot barrel pointing to the shore, the whole gun, scoured clean by 330 years of sand-blasting by the action of the waves, glinting bright gold in the filtered sunlight. It was lying on top of a sweeping bed of sand which extended for a hundred yards around. David spat out the snorkel and yelled for Gerry. Waving his arms excitedly he shouted to him to come over. Gerry, unable to hear what David was saying, ducked his head into the water and swam toward him.

Then he too stopped, his attention drawn to a glint on the seabed which on the briefest examination turned out to be another cannon. Elated, the men whooped for joy and spent several minutes paddling in the water congratulating one another before making a plan to investigate the site further. They both knew they might never have such perfect conditions for diving again – at least not for months – and that they must mark the site carefully. But they were too excited, their heads spinning with excitement, to devise any sensible scheme for some time. Making a note of their bearing from a promonotory on the shore, they swam out to sea.

"The closest gun was in eight feet, but as we swam out we just saw more and more cannon in a straight line out to sea, and we found the last one a quarter of a mile out," David recalls. "We were doing a classical zigzag pattern, crossing behind one another so as to check the same ground and at the same time cover maximum bottom space. The swimming is dangerous there because of the currents in that little bay, but we had no time to consider such comparative banalities as we went on finding cannon, a total of twenty-one in one day, which I knew was probably a world record anyway.

"I was furious for not bringing my camera with me, and frantically tried to remember the location of each cannon in relation to marker points ashore. Gerry naturally was doing the same."

When they flopped through the surf back on to the beach at Sardinia Bay they had been in the water for five hours. Exhausted, they got into the car and drove home, praying that the weather would hold so they could return the next day with a camera. From home Gerry phoned the airport weather station for a long range forecast and found that the weather would probably hold in the morning, but would almost certainly deteriorate later, with a south-easter blowing up.

Neither can recall sleeping that night, though they did not admit it until much later. Both felt that every minute of the past five years of frustration had paid off. Thoughts of all kinds flicked in and out of their minds. Would they find proof that the ship was the *Sacramento*? How? Who was there in the world who could identify the cannon positively? What were they worth? Did they intend to sell them? How would they raise the guns? What did they weigh? And so on.

Waiting only until the local chemist opened so that they could buy colour film for the Nikonos underwater cameras they drove back the next morning to Sardinia Bay. The water was appreciably rougher, but looked clean enough as they ran into the surf and battled their way out beyond the breakers, turning as soon as possible to head back towards Schoenmakerskop and the guns off Gordon's beach. They had little difficulty in locating them once they lined up the landmarks; and set about photographing them as they lay on the bottom, unable to resist the temptation to swim down and touch them, just to make sure it was not all a hoax.

Both men had decided to wear only the warm tops of their wet suits, but they had not reckoned on the wind bringing with it the stinging bluebottles which follow a south-easter off that coast as night follows day, and both were being badly stung around the legs. They decided to swim straight on to Gordon's beach and walk back to the car at Sardinia Bay.

As they waded ashore, knee deep in the water and treading carefully on the rocky bottom, they fell over Gordon's anchors – literally so in Gerry's case. But his shouts of abuse at tripping were silenced as he turned and saw what had caused him to crash down on the sharp rocks.

"We had always asked people who lived at Schoenmakers, and those who fished there regularly, if they had seen them and everyone said no. It just shows that people really don't know what they are seeing," Gerry said.

This time they felt calmer as they reviewed the find, standing there on the rocks with the wind freshening and the waves swirling about their knees, and keeping one foot on the anchors while they took bearings on the overgrown sand-dunes. Several things were now definite. They had found Gordon's wreck without a shadow of doubt. The wreck was that of a big ship, as evidence the cannons found a quarter of a mile offshore, and she had obviously struck in fairly deep water. Furthermore the evidence before them tallied precisely with Feyo's description of the *Sacramento* wreck, when he said the fatal wave struck the ship considerably offshore and she "quickly went to pieces" with the bow carried far inshore on the wave so that "of the others, who had remained in the prow, some got ashore clinging to the yards, and some to pieces of timber". Later Gerry and David also found bits of ebony as Gordon had. To them the conclusion was irresistible: they had found the *Sacramento* at last.

Later David heard from local people that from time to time a camping site had been uncovered in the bushes directly opposite the spot where the anchors lay. They also said that after frequent bushfires in the area a line of white stones could be seen leading from the site to the beach. David assumed that the survivors hoped the stones would be spotted by a passing ship which might send a boat ashore to investigate.

That night they drove home in the encroaching dark discussing what to do about the find. Gerry had to report for the army the next day, and there would have to be some rapid work that night in saying farewells and buying friends drinks; but they swore that no matter what happened neither of them would divulge the fact that they had found the *Sacramento*. Once they had salvaged as much as they humanly could they would bring in the Press and perhaps the newly established television service, but until then only those selected to work with them should be told anything at all. It would be a devilishly hard secret to keep, especially since they had picked up worn chips from the more eroded cannon to have the metal analysed; and whoever did that would want to know where it came from. A cover story would therefore have to be concocted. That night, too, they decided that David would have to carry on by himself. They could not afford to wait for Gerry's return in three months, for by then the weather would have turned and the operation would almost certainly be delayed for a year.

Before going out they discussed some ideas for lifting the guns. "Our first impression was, how the Hell do you lift something that size in the surf line? It would be very dangerous indeed to bring in a boat; but we would have to go into this in real detail before we tried anything," David commented.

Next morning Gerry left for the Angolan border, and after seeing him off David turned to the difficulties of the salvage.

Chapter 6

Before Gerry left next morning it was agreed that David should attempt the salvage alone in order to take best advantage of the remaining good weather for the year. At a calm look the problems he faced appeared insurmountable: he had little or no money; no boat; and no idea how to lift what he estimated to be two to three tons of cannon apiece. But he pondered the problems and slowly eliminated them, starting by deciding that the only means of lifting the cannon would be from a powerful and fast boat small enough to back right into the dangerous surf line, yet big enough to carry up to four or five guns at a time. He also realised that the standard technique of using lifting bags or "camels" was out of the question. (Camels are bags attached to the object by a wire strop, and filled under water from a compressed air supply so that they rise to the surface carrying with them the object to be lifted. Strop is a nautical term for a lifting loop, originally made of rope with its ends spliced to form a circle.) In the pounding surf a three-ton cannon would be lethal once it broke free of the bottom, and any diver who went down to surpervise the operations could easily be killed. The cannon would also be bounced against the bottom in places as the waves alternately rushed up the shore and then swept back. The only feasible system was to break the cannon free of the sand; then, by using a powerful boat, it would be possible to carry them underwater suspended from wire strops and so take them to deeper and calmer waters where they could be lifted later several at a time. (According to the Maritime Museum at Greenwich this was a unique idea, and somewhat ironic, in that the cannon would be lifted clear of the bottom only to be dumped again in even deeper water.)

While working out the detail David spent considerable time reviewing the boats and crews at his disposal. Not many would do. There are usually few boats of substance in Port Elizabeth harbour, and those which are there tend to be full-time fish trawlers which cannot be hired. The choice therefore narrowed rapidly to one, the thirty-five foot twin engined, single hulled pleasure cruiser *Marlin* owned and skippered by Arthur Perry. She was home-built, but a sturdy sea boat with equipment capable of heavy lifts.

Arthur Perry is a delightfully impish man with twinkling eyes who wears a sea captain's cap at a jaunty angle and is usually up to his elbows in engine grease. One way and another he had spent most of his working life at or near the sea, and had worked for some time at the Museum Oceanarium with its tame performing dolphins. It was his wife Muriel Rowe who helped catch the first pair of dolphins and so brought the Oceanarium to international fame. White haired, buxom and capable of looking after herself in any situation, Muriel always went to sea with her husband, cooking, steering, and often fishing along with him, or advising fishing parties who sailed with them. Both were used to the rough and tumble of life on the fishing jetty, the vagaries of the often drunk coloured seamen, the Indian fish-and-chip shop owners out to make a fast couple of pounds at every turn, and the wary customs officers and policemen keeping a hawk's eye on all the activity.

The matter of secrecy was constantly in David's mind. Having examined the situation carefully he realised that the need for secrecy was two-fold: he had to acquire a licence from the customs officials before he could go near the wreck with a view to salvage; and he could not afford – nor did he wish – his find to be poached by other diving teams who would be keen to cash in once they knew that the valuable guns had been found.

He went to see Arthur, and showed him the underwater pictures together with the bronze samples which had by now been certified as high quality bronze*. Arthur agreed at once to join the venture with *Marlin*, but he was not a rich man and could not afford to give his services. David knew this, and it was agreed that the *Marlin* would be hired at the commercial rate once he was able to find sponsors. Luckily that proved far less of a problem than finding the right boat and captain; two local businessmen, George Swain, a retired Royal Naval officer, and Harry Toon, a garage owner retired from the Royal Air Force, were delighted to advance 6,000 rands against an agreed share of any future profits.

Delighted at the success he was having, David went to see the customs officials and deposited 2,000 rands for a licence to work the *Sacramento*, together with the ordinary stipulation that Customs would receive fifteen per cent of the value of recovered property. He set off eagerly next day to buy wire rope to make the strop he knew would be necessary, as well as rope, buoys for marking the cannon, and other gear which Arthur did not have to hand. Almost ready to go to sea for the first time, David sat down to consider the problem of breaking the cannon free from the sand and rock bottom. He knew that most of the cannon had become attached to the rocky bottom because of a calcium build-up during the 330 years under water. They were also in most cases covered with a shell and sand encrustation as well. It would therefore need some force to break the guns loose – and in addition some of the cannon were buried up to eight feet in the sand. Ruling out explosives as a barbarous method of excavation to be used only by "scrap metal merchants", he decided to make a giant pair of plate steel pincers weighing fifty pounds. He hoped the pincers could be put in place round the cannon barrels and pulled tight by ropes tied to the end of each pincer. It would then be up to *Marlin*'s engines and the momentum of the surf to get the guns free. As a fail-safe he had a second idea which would take longer if it had to be used. This was a giant forty-pound steel hook which could be slid into the barrel once he had cleared it of sand and concretion by using a crowbar. The idea would be to use the *Marlin* to break the cannon free with the hook, and then to fit a steel strop round the gun and move it to the storage area in forty feet of water.

With few working days when the weather was suitable, David had been using all his spare time to swim over the site and measure the cannon one by one, noting their exact location against shore markers. He also found a suitable reef on which there was little sand to cover the cannon to serve as a storage area.

On February 23, after only three weeks of preparation, David and Arthur stealthily loaded the wire strops, air bottles and other equipment aboard *Marlin* at dead of night. As much of the gear as possible was stowed out of sight below decks. A crew sworn to secrecy had already been selected, and after midnight David sat aboard *Marlin* and told Arthur the exact site they would be working on, and how he proposed to go about the job. They had already selected two deckhands, Cyril Gradwell and Gerry Shultz, and both were also sworn to secrecy. Gradwell, a strapping man, was a keen diver and suitable for doing heavy work in what would certainly be dangerous, and perhaps unpleasant, conditions.

The next morning the crew, David excepted, boarded *Marlin* as if about to put to sea on a normal fishing expedition. Too well known for his salvage activities to be seen by the fishermen who might follow *Marlin* to sea, David woke early and drove quickly to Sardinia Bay, where he

*A breakdown of the bronze showed that it was constituted as follows: 0.01% zinc; 0.08% antimony; 1.4% iron; 1.7% lead; 9.2% tin; 87% copper

---

(above) Gerry van Niekerk inspects just some of the huge cannon salvaged from the *Sacramento*.
(below) Ten tons of cannon are loaded aboard the trawler *Etosha*. The long "land" guns, up to 18 feet in length, are in the foreground while the crew prepare to lower a more stubby "naval" gun to the deck.

parked and set off along a bush track to Gordon's beach and the wreck site. He had three hours at least before Arthur would arrive, and wanted to attach buoys to the cannon he thought they could lift that day. His full diving gear was aboard *Marlin*, so using only his snorkel he swam out, and was disappointed to find that visibility was only two or three feet. But he was able to mark three cannon and then swim far out to sea to await Arthur's arrival.

Once *Marlin* had arrived Arthur backed her gingerly into the surf and the pincers were lowered to David. They proved useless at once. He turned instead to the hook and eventually got into a barrel of one of the cannon. Then came the most heartbreaking disappointment. No sooner had Arthur felt two tugs on a light line between him and David which meant he could go ahead, than *Marlin*'s engines spluttered and failed. To David, unaware of this at first and still underwater, there was a brief moment of ecstasy as the cannon broke loose and surged forward on its hook; but after a hundred yards it stopped, and he surfaced to find Arthur cursing his engines and hastily making repairs so as to get clear of the area. Reluctantly they decided to abandon the effort to raise any guns and returned to port for a bitter-sweet party at which no one was prepared to believe that the cannon had moved at all – more from a sense of total failure than because they disbelieved David.

The next suitable day after the boat was repaired was March 7. The same clandestine procedure was carried out, and *Marlin* arrived on the site. David's log, though terse, records the events of the day. "Dive number 506; temperature warm; weather excellent; visibility twenty feet; bottom reef and sand. Used barrel hook on cannon nearer to shore. Broke it loose, stropped, and towed into deep water pile. Duration of dive thirty minutes." Put in that clinical way it sounds child's play. The reality was far from it. Using their code of tugs on a light line to keep in touch, Arthur and David had a hair-raising time of it. The cannon came loose easily enough as Arthur gunned the engines to full speed ahead (and closed his eyes in case anything parted or his boat fell apart under the power and pounding of the surf). But underwater David, who had to hold the barrel hook in place, suddenly found he had to deal with a three and a half ton bronze cannon swivelling wildly in the surf. To add to the trouble he was in the direct line of the turbulence from *Marlin*'s propellors, which rose and crashed just above his head in the shallow water. Clinging to the three-quarter inch steel cable of the strop, David managed to get the cannon ready for moving. He attached the rope to the strop so that Arthur could move ahead and gave two tugs on the line for Go ahead. The cannon surged forward, took the top off a rock on the bottom – and sliced through the three inch nylon rope inches above where David was holding it. As the cannon crashed to the bottom he saw that part of it had corroded and, with over three centuries of sand blasting by grains suspended in the surf, had been given a razor sharp cutting edge. This had fouled the rope and sliced it. But David found a place on the barrel where the strop could be placed, and the cannon was moved underwater almost half a mile out to sea.

During the next eight hours underwater he stropped and moved four cannons to the deep water storage place, prepared a fifth for lifting, and using a hammer and chisel together with his crowbar cleared a further three for the next attempt. The log for that day continues with the second dive, number 507: "Worked number three cannon and dug hole under barrel and stropped. Began to tow, and had fantastic battle until we moved tow to centre of the boat. Felt sudden release and moved to drop-off point." Later he recorded, "Went down to clear line from

---

The ravages of 330 years shows up clearly on these badly corroded cannon some of whose barrels have been half eaten away. (below) Underwater they have the characteristic gleam which the salvage team noted turned to a dirty green immediately the guns were brought into the air. Most of the corrosion was caused by "sand blasting" as particles of sand were washed across the guns in the swell.

propellers and found one propeller missing; this explains loss of power. Cleared line on remaining prop, and Arthur put back for harbour on one engine. Excellent day's work with four cannon in deep water and three more ready to go".

That evening's party made up for the dismal one on the previous occasion. David and the crew were elated at their success, but annoyed next day to find that the weather had deteriorated and that they would have to wait over a fortnight until March 18 for their next attempt.

On that day they set out for the site again, still in conditions of complete secrecy. This time the danger to David underwater was even greater when the ten-ton breaking-strain steel cable of the barrel hook snapped and snaked past his head as Arthur put the engines ahead. The cable could easily have beheaded him. David surfaced, told Arthur to apply the power more slowly, and took several minutes to catch his breath before diving with the spare barrel hook. The cannon they were working on was heavily encrusted but came loose after a struggle. Later they recovered an earlier cannon, that which had been moved only a short way on the first day when the engines failed; but visibility was poor and it was hard to locate the other guns inshore. During the day David went to photograph the cannon already in what had come to be called the "vault" out at sea, and for the first time took notice of the ornate dolphins and crests on them. Swimming back to the wreck site he found a ship's lead sounding line, probably from the *Sacramento*, which he used to mark the next cannon. While fitting the barrel hook to this cannon David cut his wrist badly, but was obliged to carry on because he could not afford to lose a day so good. Then another minor irritation occurred when someone aboard *Marlin* heaved the barrel hook over the side without attaching a line to it. But David found it in the end and moved the eleventh gun to the vault.

Sitting aboard *Marlin* above the vault and sipping drinks at the end of the day, David told Arthur that the first phase of the operation was now completed. The eleven guns he had found were safely below them and ready to be lifted and taken ashore. In his excitement Arthur radioed Muriel (who had not come to sea that day) "They are lying all over the bottom like matchsticks". To their horror David and Arthur later found that the highly efficient and vigilant National Sea Rescue Institute based only yards from the fishing jetty in the harbour had intercepted the message, but luckily failed to interpret it. They also found, much later, that the Institute's ten metre high speed rescue boat had swept across the wreck site, her propeller missing by only feet one of the underwater marker buoys David had laid. But now their excitement was supreme as Arthur swung the wheel and boosted the engines to head for harbour, leaving David to swim through the surf in the close of day and climb contentedly into his car to drive home.

That night, weary but keen to press ahead, Arthur, David and the crew met to discuss their plans, and to tell a local news photographer, Evert Smith, to stand by any day to go to sea with them. Evert and Arthur frequently drank together, and Evert had been told of the project by Arthur after the first four guns had been moved. David adopted a philosophic attitude when he realised that Evert knew what they were doing. Fortunately he knew the good-humoured Evert to be one of the most discreet of the local journalists. A big, bluff man with a pitch black moustache. Evert had a quick wit and easy going manner, and David decided that he could be trusted. He was in any case told by Arthur that there would be no problem.

David told Evert that he should tell the story to a trustworthy reporter so that once they had hired a suitable trawler for the heavy lifting work they could set off immediately. David wanted the event recorded for history, so he telephoned the embryonic South African Broadcasting Television service that night too, and later met a senior member of the service whom he invited to be present at the first lift, together with a film crew.

Finding a trawler, and especially a skipper prepared to take the risks involved, did not prove easy. When the first man approached was told of the approximate site of the wreck he said it would be far too dangerous; a second skipper wanted special insurance. On a Saturday night, even by using every contact he had in the business world, David simply could not arrange it. He abandoned the attempt for that weekend and disconsolately went on interviewing trawler owners.

The need for secrecy was now to some extent irrelevant because the newspaper and television men would be with them anyway, but David and Arthur still exercised discretion in case anyone tried to pirate the wreck before they could mount their own expedition. Eventually they met Gerrit Botha who owned the stout green-hulled trawler, *Etosha*. Gerrit (known as Gert) soon agreed to a charter, but insisted that the hire rate would be 500 rands a day. To David and his backers this seemed a reasonable sum in view of the conditions they were asking him to sail in. In addition they would be steaming for six hours a day. But for David personally it meant that he would be under added pressure to ensure that there were no foul-ups. One day lost would be a severe financial setback; and he would not have many – if any – more to play with. It had to go right and he had to do it, for David had throughout been the only diver under water, and only he had gained experience in stropping and controlling the cannon. The responsibility was his alone. Arthur and the crew were a major part of the team, but there was nothing they could do unless he had done his job thoroughly. Furthermore he would be "on camera" with the television teams only too eager for the drama a mistake could yield. For the next few nights he therefore lost a lot of sleep going over and over again exactly how he would run the operation.

Once again all the diving and lifting equipment was put aboard *Etosha* secretly, though the next morning anyone on the fishing jetty who suspected that Arthur and David were up to something had their suspicions confirmed as the television men moved their equipment down the jetty in the early morning. For Gradwell it was a field day. Although he had not been asked to do any diving he had brought a wet suit bottom specially, and proceeded to flex his muscles and even scale the mast for the cameras, amid howls of derisive laughter from Arthur and his wife who knew him so well. For David this was the tensest moment of all. Once they were at sea he would be in his element and totally committed to going ahead; but now there were so many last minute decisions to take and things to check. He and *Etosha*'s skipper George Braxton sat huddled in the tiny wheelhouse which reeked of fish with the skipper's cubby-hole bunk at their backs and went over the plans; the signals they would use; above all, as David carefully showed George the exact site, how best to get there, and what to do in an emergency.

It was in the early dawn of March 22 that they sailed away from the fishing jetty, past the brick-red ore berth and across the mill pond of a harbour to the signal station, where George slowed to ask permission to leave harbour. Then they turned to starboard and with mist low on the gently rolling sea gained speed, running past the Port Elizabeth seafront with its bathing beaches, hotels and wealthy suburbs, heading for Cape Recife. Aboard *Etosha* that morning were George Swain and Harry Toon who had put their money into the project, Gert Botha who would not miss the trip for worlds, Arthur and Muriel Perry, Cyril Gradwell, Gerry Shultz, and another volunteer deckhand. From the Press came Evert Smith with his Nikon cameras safe from salt spray in their familiar steel cases, and Geoff Bird, senior reporter of the *Evening Post* for which paper both men worked. There were also the television team and two Africans. In the trawler's cabin, carefully laid on ice at the instructions of Harry Toon and George Swain, were several bottles of champagne.

It is awkward to round Cape Recife in mist. There are projecting reefs, and as you get past the lighthouse and turn almost due east for Gordon's beach there is a reef known as Thunderbolt which usually breaks in all weathers. It is just possible to sneak between Thunderbolt and the shore, but woe betide the skipper who judges the gap badly. That morning in March, George gave Thunderbolt a wide berth, thereby adding time to the trip, but making certain that he got safely to Gordon's beach. They passed down the coast, which from Cape Recife changes first to a magnificent long sweep of the purest white sand, then to rocks and a small rise to the coastal road, then farther eastwards to thickly wooded coast, until they reached the cliffs at Schoenmakerskop. As the crew breakfasted they could smell the heather and bracken which on good days one can smell several miles out to sea – at night local skippers often use the smell as a rough measure of how far they are off shore. For David the three hour trip was interminable, with *Etosha* rolling as George ran parallel to the coast and the waves came at her on the beam.

Daylight grew. The sun rose fast, casting a shimmer over the water. The temperature rose slightly, dispelling the mist. And all the time there was the mesmerising beat of the trawler's diesel engine. Eventually, standing next to George in the wheelhouse, David gave the order to stop so he could line up his shore markers and manoeuvre the boat close to the vault.

The plan was to use the *Etosha*'s trawl warp and heavy lifting gear, not over the stern as is usual when fishing, but over the side, and rigged from the mast in such a way that the cannon could be kept away from the boat's side – an over-riding fear was that a sudden big wave could send one of the heavy cannon crashing through the trawler's wooden hull.

David's diving log notes: "Dive number 531. Water temperature icy; visibility 15 feet, weather, misty/fair. Went out on trawler for first lift. Dropped marker, and I went down and located the cannon and buoyed them. Moved boat into position for first lift. Duration of dive 15 minutes at 40 feet."

David surfaced and then, with the steel strops and cable dived again, closely watched from the deck where the television cameras whirred and Evert clicked away with his still cameras. He was determined to move slowly, precisely and efficiently as he went towards the first cannon. He had decided to use two strops on each gun to give it greater stability as it was winched up, "I could not use gloves as I normally would, because in the murky water I needed that sense of feel so that I could be sure that everything was correctly joined" said David later. "I found as I worked with the steel wire rope that my hands were getting badly cut, but there seemed no help for that. I got the two strops around the first gun by burrowing through the sand under it. In fact it was just a barrel, the rest having corroded away, but I thought it would provide a good test of our capability before we tried to lift any of the better-preserved guns. Then I attached the strops to the main steel rope by shackle." He used his underwater camera to photograph the cannon on the bottom before surfacing, and told George and Arthur to go ahead with the lift.

Etosha lurched over on her side as the huge barrel broke free of the bottom. The mast, which took much of the weight, groaned and creaked in protest. George and Gert Botha were worried that it might break as the winches slowly wound in the steel rope and the barrel rose to the surface. As it lifted above the surface to whoops of delight from the entire crew, the barrel changed colour dramatically as oxidation took place. From being bright blue underwater it suddenly went green before the television cameras while the crew hauled it clear of the gunwales and inboard to be laid out on deck. This colour change became a feature of all lifts.

Both the skipper and owner of *Etosha* were having serious doubts about going on with the lifts. Neither they nor David had realised that the cannon would weigh anything like this. Furthermore the swell was increasing and a strong current was pushing *Etosha* inshore. Gert told David he was not happy. If a barrel alone weighed so much – perhaps three tons, he thought – how much would a whole gun weigh? David said he was keen to try another. Reluctantly Gert and George agreed.

For his next lift David chose one of the whole, but badly corroded, cannon. Again it took fifteen minutes of work underwater before he surfaced and shouted for the lift to start. His log notes: "Pulled second cannon on to gunwale, and skipper and owner very dubious about more lifts as current and swell strong. Lowered the gun on to deck and decided to try for another."

David felt the tension which had built up in him drain away. It was replaced by sheer elation. He had proved that the cannon could be lifted comparatively easily, and whatever happened now they had secured two, albeit in bad condition, to show the sceptics ashore. The remainder of the crew could hardly contain themselves throughout the morning. The *Etosha* was alive with their expressions of joy. Yet the best was yet to come. David decided to go for one of the better preserved of the guns, and swam down with the strops to secure it. He made absolutely sure of what he was doing. The dive took thirty minutes including putting strops around the breach. When it came aboard the gun proved that he had found the *Sacramento*. Quite clearly visible on the dripping barrel were the crest of Portugal and the legend that the gun had been cast by A. G. Feyo, a gunsmith in Portugal not related to the diarist. (It has been shipped to Goa and mounted in the *Sacramento* in 1635.) What is more, there was still a fibrous fuse in the touch hole of the gun*.

Frozen with the cold water, but unable to contain his excitement, David went down for a fourth cannon which was also found to bear the Portuguese crest. By now George and Gert had overcome their nervousness and were as excited as everyone else aboard. The decision to lift a fifth and last cannon for the day was mutual. That safely aboard, they decided that it would be unseamanlike to load *Etosha* any further for the long trip to port. David dived to recover the marker buoys while George ordered the anchor to be raised.

As he hauled himself over the side for the last time David was sprayed with champagne as Harry Toon and George Swain cracked open the bottles. While David was underwater someone had swum inshore to collect oysters so that as George turned for home in the setting sun with the boat now low in the water, and rolling slowly in the swells with the weight of the cannon, they ate oysters, drank champagne and talked excitedly about the five huge guns lying on the deck.

Next day the *Evening Post* gave three-quarters of its front page to the find. Headlined *Historical East Cape Find*, Geoff Bird's story began "Eleven bronze cannon dating back to before Van Riebeeck's arrival at the Cape were recovered yesterday from the site of what is believed to the be the wreck of the once proud Portuguese galleon, *Sacramento*, off the Eastern Cape coast." (Of the twelve cannon in the vault, only five had in fact been brought ashore, leaving seven there for the meantime.) Bird continued, "The re-location of the wreck and the recovery of the cannon . . . is the most significant marine archaeological discovery ever off the South African coast. It is also believed to be the greatest number of bronze cannon found at the site of a wreck anywhere in the world. The value of the find in financial and historical terms cannot at present be determined . . . There were cheers from those on board the trawler as the boat derrick creaked and groaned under the terrific weight and finally brought the first cannon to the surface . . . Mr Allen's perseverance in finding the cannon in an extremely dangerous area and the feat in lifting them from the seabed with the minimum of problems is regarded as 'fantastic'."

That night David and Arthur used a low-loading lorry to transport the guns to Arthur's home where they were immediately put on public display.

*When David and Gerry examined the guns carefully on a later occasion they were surprised to find that some were actually loaded. Boxer, equally surprised, speculated that the *Sacramento* might have spotted a possible enemy sometime during the storm and was cleared for action. The true explanation was however supplied by Lieut-Commander Peter Whitelock MBE, captain of *HMS Victory* in Portsmouth, who said that it was a frequent practice to keep guns loaded at sea, and one which proved irritating to the gunners because they had to keep the powder dry by drawing the shot and replacing it at frequent intervals. The idea was to have "one up the spout" in case of surprise attack.

Chapter 7

That same night the South African television news led with the story of the *Sacramento* and David found himself plunged into a whirl of publicity, newspaper rivalry and its attendant jealousies. What was worse, he soon became embroiled in an attempt by others to salvage the guns for themselves.

The *Evening Post*'s first edition reaches the rival morning paper *The Eastern Province Herald* just before mid-day. The first person there to see it, naturally enough, was the news editor, John Edmunds. He must have been furious when he saw the banner headlines in the *Post*, for he had trained David's brother for five years, at the end of which time he was appointed on secondment to the paper's London bureau where he then was. To be scooped in these circumstances was unpalatable. David's hurried phone call to explain that he had been barn-stormed into events by Arthur Perry, who told Evert Smith of the find first, could have done little to relieve the bitterness of the moment. However the *Herald* recovered next morning with a page three story and pictures of the cannon ashore.

The story sounded the first warnings of possible poaching, and as such was to prove prophetic. It read, "The team who salvaged 11 cannon from a wreck in Algoa Bay near Port Elizabeth, this week intend to explore the area further, but they will not say where it is or what they hope to find". In the circumstances it was not surprising that the *Herald* incorrectly placed the wreck in Algoa Bay, but Bird's mistaken report that eleven cannon had already been recovered, though perhaps true in the sense that David knew where they were, was perpetuating itself. The story went on, "Leader of the team, Mr David Allen, said the reason for their secretiveness was the danger of other licensed salvagers 'poaching' on their find. They hoped to get some form of protection against other salvagers. Mr John Wiley, MP for Simonstown, and an expert on maritime affairs, was coming to Port Elizabeth to discuss this with them. . . . The Port Elizabeth historian Mr Alf Porter said the discovery was historically invaluable and the most important in South Africa this century."

For his afternoon edition Bird had little more to go on, but the *Post* again ran a front page picture and story quoting the Portuguese consul in Port Elizabeth, Mr John Vieira, on the importance of the discovery. By now the story had spread nationally and people were flocking to Arthur Perry's home to view the five cannon on display in his garden. David's home phone rang constantly with media and public inquiries. From Simonstown the chief of the South African Navy, Vice-Admiral J.J. Johnson, expressed interest and later took the opportunity when on a visit to Port Elizabeth to inspect the cannon and offer the Navy's facilities in designing a gun carriage.

David wrote in haste to Gerry to tell him of the recovery of the guns, and made plans to retrieve the remainder as soon as the weather moderated and he was able to sail again. The first opportunity came on Monday March 28 when in thick mist and freezing cold water he and the

---

Carrying out preservation work on a cannon sold to the Port Elizabeth museum. Gerry cleans the ornate touch hole. Note the white barnacles and sea growth on the as yet uncleaned muzzle of the gun. The steel structure was used so that the clean part of the gun could be kept under canvas covers in bad weather.

crew aboard *Etosha* raised the remaining seven cannon with little fuss, taking three-quarters of an hour over each lift. They also found the longest of the guns, seventeen feet from breech to muzzle; and returned, still in mist, to find the television crew waiting on the jetty together with the hired low-load trailer to take the cannon to Arthur's home. Once again Bird got the beat on the story and quoted Harry Toon as saying that the cannon would be sold once they had been properly examined by various museums and historical bodies.

David soon became aware that some people involved in the project, and even some not closely connected, had caught treasure fever, believing as they stared at the cannon that they were looking at an instant fortune. "It's an extraordinary phenomenon" David commented. "People see or hear about treasure and they become devious and greedy in the desire to make a quick fortune. Most often refer to 'treasure' in the wrong sense anyway, for as far as I am concerned treasure consists of pieces of eight and gold. Cannon, compasses, and trading goods are artefacts, more to be kept and examined and put in their historical context than to be sold for a fast few pounds. But quite ordinary people behave in the most despicable way once they have become gripped by the desire for treasure. Naturally I got excited as well, and of course I knew that we could make money out of what we had, but for me there were other considerations – mainly the historical importance and the sense of my own achievement – which I was not prepared to minimise. Having studied the records thoroughly I knew that I had recovered more cannon from one site than any one of the most famous names in marine archaeology. Furthermore Gerry and I had not required a big team, expensive equipment, or even much fuss to do it."

At this point in the story a Cape Town diver named Brian Clark, who mainly salvages and sells metal for scrap, was tipped off for 2,500 rands about the position of the site and told that there were more bronze cannon to be salvaged. He at once left Cape Town in his converted trawler *Gavin* with his two crew members Peter Mason and Brian MacFarlane to take advantage of the situation. Armed with his own salvage licence he could go ahead and lift whatever was left on the bottom.

Beside himself with anger, David went to work to neutralise the danger. He devised a plan to absorb Clark's team into his own, a scheme which eventually cost him 23,000 rands and called a meeting at which lawyers representing himself, Harry Toon and the Clark team would be present. Clark himself was not to be there. The meeting finally produced an agreement so advantageous to David that Clark later expressed amazement that he had, through his lawyer, signed it.

In the agreement Clark undertook to stay off the site. David would hire Clark's crew and boat and use them, together with the *Etosha*, to recover the cannon lying in the surf line. The smaller and more manoeuvrable *Gavin* would run right into the surf and the cannon would be slung underneath her, then ferried out to the *Etosha* standing out to sea where they could be lifted at once. If Clark and his men wanted action, David thought, they would get it in the surf. By now his anger was dissipating. To his knowledge there were only twenty-one cannon which he and Gerry had seen and marked on the site, eleven of which were already ashore and safe from any claim by Clark.

On April 18, the combined teams were ready to try for the inshore cannon. It was decided that in this first combined operation, during which Clark's men accustomed themselves to the area, the *Etosha* would not be used. Arthur Perry would sail in the *Gavin* to give instructions on

---

Moving the cannon is an expensive and problematic process. For each move special heavy lift mobile cranes and heavy-duty vehicles are need. Here David swings the finely balanced "miracle cannon" as it is lifted from its temporary mounting to be moved elsewhere.

getting to the site, while David and Brian MacFarlane – or Mac, as he was known – would swim off the beach and mark the buoys before the trawler arrived. They parked the car at Sardinia Bay and battled through the pounding surf. It took an hour to get to Gordon's beach, where they started marking the cannon they thought could be most easily picked up. This done, David told Mac to wait on the site while he swam out to sea to guide the trawler in through the reefs – a task which he knew would be difficult and hazardous.

As he swam, head underwater, scanning the familiar bottom, David's eye was caught by the glint of a badly scoured cannon. He stopped, went over the site in his mind, and looked up to check the shore markings. It was impossible – there couldn't be a cannon here, for he and Gerry had searched the whole area. Then he checked the shore markers again and found he was much farther out to sea than before, perhaps half a mile off the beach, and in deeper water. He dived to the cannon and stopped as he approached it. There before him was the find of the century – thirty cannon packed neatly breech to muzzle, exactly as they had been in the hold of the *Sacramento*. If he was ever in danger of drowning it was now. He almost forgot to clench the snorkel in his teeth as he let out a quickly stifled Whoop!

Trying to keep calm although his body was tensed with excitement, he swam slowly across the hold counting the number of guns – thirty. "Now" he thought "I really have done it. This will certainly go down in history." But even in those few minutes as the last of the air in his lungs was exhausted, what was uppermost in his mind was that here was the final proof that the wreck was the *Sacramento*. Feyo's description of the wrecking raced through his brain ". . . rising on a great wave she struck from stern to stern and quickly went to pieces". It was clear to David that the entire hold had simply dropped out as the great ship smashed down on the bottom, her planking ripped from her with the combined weight of the cargo and the giant's fist of a wave slamming her on to the sand*. Feyo had continued, ". . . seeing there was no further hope (the chief captain and many others) withdrew to the galleries to confess themselves; and only one of them escaped. Of the others, who had remained in the prow, some got ashore clinging to the yards, and some to pieces of timber . . ."

Exactly, David thought; once the ship's hold was torn from her, the upper part must have disintegrated almost at once; only the prow, with perhaps some parts of the upper deck, were carried on by the following waves into the shallows where they were dumped, depositing the forward ship's cannon and the anchors where he had found them. Other mounted cannon had clearly fallen through the gun deck between the first strike and the shore.

The cannon (thought David) had been identified as Portuguese. There was, too, the evidence of the camp site and the anchors. No further proof was needed to show that this was the *Sacramento*. As he kicked his flippers to swim to the surface he could see the *Sacramento* riding on the back of that giant wave, her crew in a frenzy of religious despair, her sails torn by the wind, until with a keel-breaking crack she smashed down and fell to bits. That she had struck here, half a mile off shore in perhaps fifty feet of water, was indeed an indication of the size of the galleon. And as David reached the surface he had no doubt that beneath him were Feyo's guns of China, and Bocarro's guns from Macao.

"I'm told that as I reached the surface I had the snorkel out yelling to Mac to bring marker buoys, trying to attract the attention of the boat and swimming apparently in three directions at once," David said. Aboard *Gavin* this startling performance was taken as a sign that David had at the least been confronted by a shark – or judging by the violence of his reaction, more probably an unknown sea monster. The skipper swung the wheel and opened the throttles, heading toward him at speed. "You don't have to go any farther, stop here," David yelled.

*The echo sounder "trace" of the rock the ship struck is given on the site plan illustration.

David recorded the find in his log: "Saw a huge cannon ahead of me. As I swam over it I found about 30 cannon (laid out as in the hold) on the bottom; nearer to the shore in 50 feet were another six."

It was the work of seconds to calculate that with the weather deteriorating and the sea becoming rougher all the time, it would be safer and quicker to leave the inshore cannon and start lifting the new ones. David and Mac scrambled aboard the *Gavin*, donned their full diving gear and made a closer inspection. Beneath the neatly stacked cannon they found a piece of teak from the ship's planking – the final proof, if it was still needed, that the ship was the *Sacramento*. Then (or later) they also found peppercorns all round the cannon and even in the barrels of the guns, in a state of such perfect preservation that David's mother was prevailed on to use them in her household cooking. To her amazement she lived. The pepper had clearly burst from its sacks – as it did aboard the *Atalaya*, where according to Feyo it jammed the pump intakes. The *Sacramento* pepper eventually found its way to Europe – its original destination – in a jumbo jet, when David brought some to London to present to Boxer.

After searching the whole of the area and making mental notes on exactly where each of the outlying guns lay, they stropped up a gun heavily encrusted with red bait (a local kind of crustacean). In the growing swell it was lifted just clear of the bottom – when the winch aboard the *Gavin* jammed. Once the crew had freed it the cannon was lowered gently to the bottom and a smaller one was stropped on to the lifting cable. The gun was completely encrusted and it was only when it broke the surface that David could see that it was an iron gun.

David had long since decided to leave all iron guns in the sea because they tended to crumble rapidly when exposed to the air and there is as yet no quick and efficient way of preserving them. It would be criminal to salvage even one iron gun in South Africa where there are no facilities for preserving it. David gave the order for the gun to be lowered to the bottom, where it still remains together with sixteen other iron cannon from the *Sacramento*.

After the fiasco with the winch, and some difficulty in lifting the iron gun, David became disillusioned with the *Gavin*'s capabilities, particularly when he considered the quick and efficient team work established aboard the well-found *Etosha* once George Braxton and Gert Botha had got used to the groans and creaks of their mast, and had discovered just how much punishment the equipment could safely take. He decided to try a third lift, this time selecting a big bronze gun. It almost knocked the *Gavin*'s gunwales off as it was slung inboard. The trawler heeled over perilously, water licking across the deck to within inches of the hold. Had she gone over a few inches more the boat would undoubtedly have turned turtle, possible killing some of the crew as she went. With great effort the cannon was eventually slung across the deck.

As the *Gavin* turned for the tiresome return voyage David swam ashore. Before he got into his car to drive back to Port Elizabeth he examined the pieces of wood he had recovered. They were teak and ebony – teak from the hull, ebony which would have been used for dunnage to stack the guns, and then possibly sold in Portugal to make rosaries and crucifixes.

As he drove home David made up his mind that the *Gavin* was useless for his purposes, although he would be obliged under the terms of the contract to use it again the next day.

For once the weather, which had been fair the day before, improved slightly instead of deteriorating and David sailed aboard the *Gavin* next morning for the site. Once there he went down to photograph the cannon where they lay. Visibility was poor and in the event the pictures showed little. In heavy seas they moved six of the inshore guns to deep water. David decided that there was no point in tackling the guns from the hold until the *Etosha*, which was out fishing, returned. The *Gavin* was not able to do the job, but she could still be used for ferrying the guns. The day's work was unremarkable. As the *Gavin* started for port they spotted the

Etosha coming up fast from the south-west. They waited until she came abreast, when David swam over to get a basket of soles. Aboard *Gavin* they cooked the tasty fish, caught that morning by *Etosha*, on the quaint coal burning brazier aboard the trawler. With the sun setting in a blaze of red and the muzzle of one cannon sticking out of the hold (a badly eroded seventeen foot cannon, the only one brought aboard that day) David felt extremely contented, not least because he had seen a way clear to getting rid of Clark. His log noted, "Collected soles from Gert for supper. Got dark off Schoenies and we fried soles on the way home. Got into port about 9pm – good day. We now have 13 guns in port and six in the vault."

Since Clark's arrival there had a been a re-alignment of loyalties among the Press. Bird, for example, seemed to have thrown in his lot with Clark. This annoyed David in view of the fact that he had allowed Bird his original scoop. Furthermore the *Herald* had quoted a resident of Schoenmakerskop who said, without any evidence, that David must have used explosives to get the guns free of the bottom. Tired as a result of his concerted and sustained expenditure of energy, and resenting the *Herald* report and what he interpreted as Bird's attitude, David became terse with the Press and took to saying "no comment" in place of his previously helpful statements. "Naturally I had held back quite substantial parts of the story from both papers, but I had to protect the site in the first instance and in the second I found myself willy-nilly attached to the *Post*, so that the *Herald* started giving me a caning. I finally decided that it was too bad if the Press became alienated in the meantime," David said.

On April 20 the following caption appeared in the *Post* under a front-page picture of David handling the cannon as it was being lifted ashore from the *Gavin*: "The longest, heaviest and best preserved cannon recovered so far from the site of the wreck of the *Sacramento* is brought ashore from the salvage vessel, *Gavin*, in the Port Elizabeth harbour. The cannon, which carries the Portuguese crest, is more than 4.5 metres long and weighs an estimated four tons. It was recovered by the Cape Town salvage team led by a professional diver, Mr Brian Clark. They are assisting the Port Elizabeth salvage team to recover a further 10 cannon located at the site of the wreck."

Having seen an early edition of the paper David went to confront Clark. His boat, he told him, was utterly inadequate even for an amateur and could not fulfil the conditions of the contract. A blazing row ensued with harsh words exchanged by each side. It was soon settled by a third party, the Port Elizabeth marine surveyor who inspected the *Gavin* and declared her unseaworthy. He said she must remain in port until a list of defects was put right. David, however, was on the brink of becoming entangled in an even fiercer though less vocal row on an academic level.

With fifteen guns ashore, and some breathing space while the argument over the *Gavin* continued, he called a meeting of local organisations interested in the salvage. Represented at the meeting were the Port Elizabeth Museums, the Historical Society, the Library; and the Portuguese Consul. It was readily agreed that an ad hoc historical committee should be formed under the chairmanship of Dr John Scott, a local school principal who was a member of both the Historical Society and the Museum Board. With him would be the consul, Mr Vieira; Hans Huisman, the harbour engineer, and a member of the Museum board; Dave Wratten a freelance researcher, and handy at sketching; Dr John Wallace, the director of the Museum; Alf Porter, the chief librarian; and Mrs Dee Nash, a member of the museum staff; who acted as secretary. It was agreed that Mrs Nash should write to authorities in Europe and elsewhere describing the find and asking for comment and pointers to identification. At this juncture David had no doubt at all that the wreck was that of the *Sacramento*, frequently said so, and after describing his evidence continued to refer to it as such. However Mrs Nash was not apparently satisfied.

In the meantime the arrangement seemed pleasant and workable. Dr Scott, a tall, straight-backed former Royal Marine, would collate the information as it came in and keep David informed. That settled, David returned to the problem of Clark and his boat. He had decided to continue using *Etosha* whether Clark liked it or not. Clark did not, and hostilities warmed up. On April 24, David was ready to go to sea once again in the *Etosha*; but Clark was one jump ahead. He sent Brian MacFarlane to see the Port Captain, Captain Heyns, to argue that the *Etosha* was not licensed to salvage, only to fish, and that she should be held in port. As he came abreast of the Port Captain's office Gert Botha, now acting as his own skipper, slowed as usual and contacted the signal tower on his radio asking permission to go to sea. There was a pause which Gert could not understand and then, much to his surprise, Captain Heyns himself came on the radio. "Go ahead and go fishing. You are going fishing aren't you?" he said. Gert wasted no time and pushed forward the bridge control throttles and spun the helm as he rounded the breakwater and headed to sea.

Once over the site the *Etosha*'s crew slipped back into the familiar routine. Aboard were Arthur and Muriel Perry, Dave Wratten, and some African deckhands. They manoeuvred the boat over the spot where the *Gavin* had left the six inshore cannons in forty-eight feet of water, and taking about an hour for each gun lifted all six aboard. David's total diving time was only two and three-quarter hours, considerably less than in the past. The operation neatly achieved they returned to port under cover of dark and, so as not to embarrass the Port Captain, unloaded the cannon and took them to Arthur's home which had by now become a temporary museum.

The next morning David could hardly believe his luck. Although there was a strong ground swell the weather was again nearly perfect; and Clark was still held in port. On the site there was a heavy swell. Arthur and David in consultation with Gert stopped *Etosha* short of the breakers, and broke out the inflatable rubber dinghy powered by outboard engines to go into the surf and mark the cannon. They dropped a marker buoy based on David's land sights. He then slipped over the side of the dinghy preparing to be towed across the area by Arthur – a technique David and Gerry had devised long since to cover the maximum ground area. But looking down, David found the marker had fallen exactly over the guns which had been in the hold of the ship. Gingerly Gert edged *Etosha* over the site just behind the breaker line and the first cannon for the day was stropped on.

The position was a dangerous one for *Etosha* throughout the lift. If any wave started to break slightly farther out than the rest no one could estimate what damage might then be done with three and a half tons of cannon tied to the boat by steel cable – or whether she would survive at all with the ungainly cannon making steering awkward, and having so little space to manoeuvre before she hit the beach. To minimise this danger David fixed a stern line from *Etosha* to one of the shoreward cannon while Gert used his engines to take the strain and keep the bows facing out to sea. They also tied a large sheet of thick rubber under the stern of the boat to stop the cannon piercing the hull if they did hit against it.

David dived and shackled up the biggest gun, which he guessed weighed well over four tons. His choice was now governed by the possibility of salving the best and biggest of the guns while Clark was unable to fulfil his part of the contract. They slowly hauled the big gun aboard. None knew it then; but this cannon, the most perfect of those yet brought up, with its elaborate scroll work and lotus bud cascabel, was one of the finest Bocarro cannon to survive. In moving the gun David also found more pieces of wood subsequently identified by the government laboratories in Pretoria as Indian teak.

Now the sea was really rough. David came aboard to discuss the position with Gert while they steamed offshore. There were breakers right on the point where the guns were held, and no possibility of anchoring *Etosha*. But Gert had confidence in the quick and smooth operation they had devised, and proposed a plan. He would run *Etosha* in astern with bows to the sea as soon as he found a gap in the breakers. David would go overboard at once and strop up a cannon. They would winch it clear of the bottom and steam out fast with it suspended beneath the boat. David gave Gert a quizzical look. "Oh boy," he thought, "and Gerry and I thought we were daring." Gert, one hand on the helm, the other clutching the throttles, turned the boat and slowly inched her in astern – a tricky manoeuvre at any time. Arthur kept his eyes peeled in case they had to move ahead hurriedly. As they reached the site David leapt into the water and swam for the bottom, stropping up in record time. The plan worked, and they lowered the cannon into sixty feet of water for re-stropping before lifting it aboard. But this hair-raising tactic had taken its toll of the gear. The "snatch" of the swell as the boat rose and fell had frayed and all but broken the steel cable – as the boat fell off the top of a wave the mast inclined towards the surface and caused a momentary slack in the cable; and then as she rose to another swell the mast would swing back suddenly, "snatching" up the whole weight of the cannon again. In any case the sea had become rougher, and one such manoeuvre a day was enough for Gert – and rightly so. Nonetheless as they headed home they all felt a surge of pride at the slick operation conducted "on the run". They now had twenty-one guns ashore.

Towards the end of April David deliberately chose a rough day to go to the site in *Etosha*. He wanted time alone to review the situation underwater and make an assessment of what was left of the wreck. Visibility was limited to three feet, but this was what he wanted because he intended to conduct a toothcomb search. With waves breaking overhead he went over the bottom. To his surprise he came across a clenched fist with the thumb pointing towards him which he thought must be the fist of a giant statue. (He later came to know it as a fertility symbol and the cascabel of a Bocarro cannon.) He gave it a tug, only to find that it came away in his hand. Held down by the weight of the fist, he walked slowly along the bottom and placed it beside a cannon so that he would find it again easily. Then, as he went back in his tracks, he saw another fist pointing up out of the sand, this time attached to a cannon. The cannon was wedged in the centre of what was left of the ship's hold, lying between a number of iron guns and jammed so that it was not touching the sea bed. Presumably because of the wave motion there was a huge hollow beneath it. From the appearance of the fist it would seem that the gun was in perfect condition, not scoured, and almost devoid of underwater growth. David surfaced and signalled to *Etosha*, which came surfing in through the breakers. The crew dropped his camera to him and a sack for the loose fist. David photographed the gun and attached a line to the bag so that the fist could be hauled up. While taking pictures he noted that the initials B.C. had been carved into the barrel of one gun. Supposing them to be those of Brian Clark, who he assumed had swum out from the beach at some stage, he photographed the barrel to add strength to his efforts, and those of John Wiley MP, to have the salvage laws altered to protect salvors once a claim had been established.

On April 28 Bird wrote the *Post* front page lead story. Under a picture of David holding aloft the clasped fist fertility symbol which he had found broken off one of the cannon, Bird wrote: "A further 20 bronze cannon dating back to before 1647 have been located at the site of what is believed to be the wreck of the Portuguese galleon, *Sacramento*, off the Port Elizabeth coast. This incredible find made by Port Elizabeth diver, David Allen, brings the total number of cannon found at the site of the wreck to 41." (It will be noted that Bird wrote "what is believed to be the wreck of the Portuguese galleon *Sacramento*".) He continued, "The total weight of the cannon is estimated at about 100 tons. Their value as scrap metal is estimated at almost 100,000 rands although they would be worth more as historical pieces." The reason for Bird's new-found doubts became clear two paragraphs lower. "The historian at the Port Elizabeth museum and person in charge of documenting finds from the wreck, Mrs Dee Nash, said the latest finds made the story of the *Sacramento* more likely. 'It does seem that the evidence is now that the cannon were being carried as cargo. I believe it is a significant find as it takes us a step nearer to identifying the ship,' she said."

David was infuriated. He had discovered the wreck; proved beyond question on conclusive evidence that it was that of the *Sacramento*; invited the co-operation of a local committee; and now found that the secretary of the committee, through inspired newspaper stories, was trying to supervise his discovery. In saying that the latest finds "made the story of the *Sacramento* more likely" she was by implication questioning his ability to identify his own discovery, and trying to set herself up as the authority on it. Relations with the museum and the committee became strained, and became even more so when the *Herald* carried a story some weeks later stating: "Official confirmation that the 40 cannon recently salvaged off the coast near Port Elizabeth came from the 17th century Portuguese galleon *Sacramento*, which sank in 1647, was announced last night by the historian at the Port Elizabeth Museum, Mrs M.D. Nash . . . Authentication of the cannon stemmed from an inscription on the best preserved of the cannon, Mrs Nash said last night. The inscription read: 'Antonio Teles Menezes, Governor of India, ordered this made in the year 1640 by Manoel Taverres Bocarro'. Contemporary Dutch reports verified that the *Sacramento* sailed from Goa in 1647, 'fully laden with the most beautiful goods . . . and in her hold came a quantity of cannon which the City of God in China sent as a present to his majesty.' "

Mrs Nash had apparently now read the documents which some time before enabled David to make an accurate and more detailed identification. Although the fact did not appear in the newspaper story, her tardy claim to identify the *Sacramento* resulted from information provided by Professor Boxer, who as we have already seen is the acknowledged world authority on this period of Portuguese history. Mrs Nash had written to Professor Boxer, who lives near Berkhamsted in Hertfordshire, and he had told her on the evidence before him that because the ship carried Bocarro cannon, she was in all probability the *Sacramento*. David was well aware that the evidence he had provided formed a sounder – and of course earlier – basis for identification than the single fact volunteered by Mrs Nash that the ship was carrying Bocarro guns in bulk.

By April 29 Clark had completed the list of repairs required by the surveyor. On that day David sailed the *Etosha* and *Gavin* together on the understanding that the crew of the *Gavin* would have a percentage of the value of the bronze if and when the cannon recovered that day were sold. Clark and his two crewmen had flown back to Cape Town, but they left their African crewman aboard together with hired hands to establish their rights.

At the site David ran inshore aboard the *Gavin* as planned. The sea was very rough, and there was only two feet of visibility in the fifty feet of water over the vault. At that depth he needed up to eighty feet of steel cable snaked down on the bottom, cable which he then had to haul across the sand in a lung-bursting effort to shackle the rope to the strops. He chose a small cannon which was successfully hauled aboard; but on the next attempt he came close to death. The "snatch" of a wave snapped the cable like a twig. A four-ton cannon came crashing down above his head – and there was only two feet of visibility. It required a dexterous twist of his body and a powerful kick of the flippers to dodge out of its path. The gun settled in a cloud of disturbed sand on the bottom and David abandoned any further attempts to dive that day.

On the first day of May, Gerry van Niekerk arrived back from the army, bursting to see the cannon and to hear what had happened. He and David talked late into the night, going over the sequence of success and bitter rows; and finally decided to go out the next day. Gerry was thrilled to be able to exchange the dusty early morning routine of the desert for an early start sailing into the sunrise.

The next morning, keyed up at being able to dive together again, they drove before dawn to the fishing jetty to board *Etosha* and sail for the site. David wanted to lift what he had come to call the "miracle" gun – the big, undamaged one he had found wedged between the iron cannon. It would be wonderful to lift it with Gerry, thus marking the culmination of their joint achievement on the wreck. By doing it with *Etosha* alone he could also exclude Clark from any claim to the gun. Underwater they used crowbars to work a strop around the gun, going carefully in order not to damage either it or the guns near it. Once the single strop was in place Gert Botha used the winch to lift the gun slowly from its resting place, moved *Etosha* away from the hold, and dropped the cannon back on to the seabed. David and Gerry stayed with the gun throughout the operation and then started re-stropping so that it could be lifted aboard. For the first time David allowed a long break so that the gun could be cleaned on deck. From the moment it broke the surface it was transparently the best of the haul. None of the crew could refrain from setting about partially cleaning it at once. Meanwhile Gerry went to work to strop the next gun for lifting while David scoured the bottom further afield in search of artefacts.

That day they lifted all the remaining bronze guns in the hold, and noted and charted the position of the remaining iron guns – which will be there for a long time to come. Later they moved the *Etosha* to the original deep water vault and lifted one of the guns which were still there. When she returned to port *Etosha* was low in the water with five cannon on deck. There remained only the troublesome inshore cannon and six still at the deep water vault to be salvaged.

On May 11 both the *Etosha* and the *Gavin* again sailed. Aboard the *Gavin* David had the inflatable dinghy. While Gerry took the *Etosha* to the deep water vault to load the remaining cannon, David went inshore with the *Gavin*. In all Gerry loaded just over twenty tons of cannon that day.

David was less successful. Going to the deepest of the shallow water cannon he made the dinghy fast to it and waited until Gerry was ready to come and help before hauling it aboard the *Gavin*. They then had seven cannon weighing a total of twenty-three tons aboard the two boats as they made the weary three-hour trip back to port. For David and Gerry the long trip was a chance to settle down in the closing dark, with soles for supper, and an opportunity to discuss in detail plans for the future.

The ornamentation and inscriptions on the Bocarro cannon are in themselves works of art. Clockwise from top left: A cherub's face shines out from the scroll work and tops a hanging pepper. Both are just below the touch-hole; (TR) The coat of arms of Macao, tops the rampant lion which was the monogram of the governor of India Antonio Telles de Menezes who ordered the guns cast in 1640. The wording of the inscription below describes the commission; (LR) The oriental, half human, lifting dolphins were designed and placed on the gun so that it could easily be lifted on to a mounting. They could also be used in conjunction with block and tackle to aim the gun; (LL) A detail of another cherub with hanging pepper. It is interesting to note that the cherubs too have oriental features.

ANTº TELESDEME
NEZESGOVºDºAINDIA
AMANDOVFAZER
NOANNODE1640

Chapter 8

David's experiences once the *Sacramento* story broke made several facts obvious for the future. They would need to find a source of income sufficient to support all their future salvage operations themselves; they would work in absolute secrecy, notifying only a limited number of statutory authorities of what they were doing; they would keep their logs more fully, and take their own pictures of any future site for release to the Press only after they were satisfied that the site was cleaned out. The deciding factor clearly was money – a problem which subsequently resolved itself.

But as the boat docked that night more immediate problems waited ashore. For a start there were mounting pressures to sell some of the cannon. Arthur Perry wanted to sell his share, and others felt it was time to get some money back on their investment. In addition Mr Wiley, who had been to see the cannon and had heard of the rumpus with Clark's team, was proposing to make a speech in Parliament suggesting changes in the salvage laws; and it was necessary for David to help prepare a case for him. The speech was given on May 17. "Recently I had the pleasure of going to Port Elizabeth to examine the wreck of the *Sacramento* . . ." Mr Wiley said. "I think I am right in saying that there is no legislation in South Africa that specifically governs wrecks. The nearest legislation that I can think of is perhaps the Museum Ordinances of the Provinces, or possibly the 1969 National Monuments Act. I want to suggest to the Honourable Minister (of Transport) the absolute necessity for legislation to be introduced to govern this situation for the reasons I am now going to give.

"First of all I think that there is a need for legislation to protect the wrecks around the South African Coast, particularly those wrecks which occurred before the steamship was firmly established as a means of transport in about 1860." Mr Wiley then outlined the situation in Western Australia and in several European states including Britain and France. He continued: "In the case of wrecks found along our coast, I believe it may be possible to formulate legislation which could afford wreck sites protection, at the same time also preserving the rights of private enterprise which has been responsible for finding so many of the wrecks that have been discovered to date around our coast. Until such times as museums or universities are capable of taking over the task and doing the necessary work themselves, the country will undoubtedly have to depend on private enterprise.

"I have two suggestions to make to the Minister in this regard. As in the case of the Western Australian Act, some body, and preferably a local seaport museum, might be appointed as a governing authority in a particular area . . . I am trying to emphasise the necessity for the establishment of a chain of maritime museums. The discovery of wrecks is only in its infancy in this country. There are something like 3,000 wrecks lying undiscovered around our coast according to the South African archives, I understand.

"The second point I wish to make is that private enterprise should under no circumstances be

---

David Allen, left, and Gerry van Niekerk make notes of details of the "miracle cannon" the most perfectly preserved of the 40 lifted from the *Sacramento* site. The cascabel (clenched fist in the centre foreground) is a sacro-magical fertility symbol used by Indian women to increase their chances of pregnancy. Note the perfect condition of the crest and inscription on the gun.

stifled. I think the danger of stifling private enterprise could be overcome by issuing permits by a governing authority. Such permits should be reasonably easily obtained on condition that a percentage of the artefacts recovered should be handed over to the museum which issues the permit; the museum then being given first choice, and the percentage arrived at on the assessed value for the payment of customs duties. As regards the artefacts that remain in the hands of the salvor, the museum should have first refusal on any artefact which the salvor may subsequently wish to offer for sale. The price could easily be mutually agreed upon.

"In conclusion let me say . . . that it is essential that historical wrecks when found, should be preserved, but that at the same time a formula should be arrived at which will not stifle private enterprise. I do not think it is necessary to go as far as the European laws. I think that the British Act of 1973 (which provides for a licensing system at the discretion of the Secretary of State and the declaration of a whole area as restricted for archaeological and artistic reasons) subject to certain modifications and qualifications, will suit our local conditions. Perhaps we could also include parts of the Western Australian Act which suit our purpose concerning the ownership, discovery and exploitation of wrecks off our coast.

"The last point I make is that if these wrecks are to be dealt with under legislation as I have suggested today, it is no use passing the legislation and then hoping that some people or authority will do something about it. The two suggestions I have made go hand in hand. If legislation is put on the Statute Book – which I believe it must be, and which I am sure the Minister will agree – then the local authorities will have to be encouraged to establish maritime museums – I am only dealing with maritime museums today – along our coasts. They must then appoint a director controlling the museum, or a trustee of the museum who will then have the authority to issue permits to people who wish to salvage wrecks; and they, the museums, will in turn have the first choice of the contents which have been salvaged. Only thereafter would the salvor be able to offer those goods which were not required by the local museum on the open market."

Considering the esoteric nature of its contents the speech was remarkably well received in a Parliament with more pressing matters of life and death to debate.

Legislation over historical salvage is a particularly vexed issue, and while Mr Wiley's suggestions are probably the most equitable, similar arrangements have led to some bizarre claims, particularly in Britain, where one Dutch wreck found off the English coast was deemed to be the property of the Dutch authorities, who were allowed first choice of the artefacts. The British authorities had second choice – and the salvor was left all but bankrupt. The difficulty is that unless the salvors have an independent income they need money to conduct operations, which even on a minor scale run into thousands of pounds sterling a day. Professor Boxer is particularly outspoken on this point. He believes that private enterprise gets a bad deal and that academic jealousies, particularly on the part of museum authorities, are absurd. "The museums never have the money to do this sort of thing, and they seem to be saying that it is better to leave a wreck underwater for all time rather than to allow someone else to salvage it," he told us. He also believes that if the situation is such that nothing can be salvaged without the use of explosives, then it is better to salvage what can be got rather than to leave everything underwater.

At the time of writing Mr Wiley is still pursuing the new legislation with a marked degree of success though no Bill has yet been formulated.

Mrs Nash, too, had not been inactive. She had written to a number of contacts abroad, the most notable being Professor Boxer, but declined to pass on the full information to David. Letters from Boxer were photocopied but with his address carefully cut off the head of his notepaper – a precarious precaution, because his address appears in *Who's Who* and doubtless other works of reference. It was in fact as a result of consulting *Who's Who* that Geoffrey Allen was later enabled to visit the professor – a move which the former understands was not to the lady's liking. Perhaps it should be added that Professor Boxer had written to Mrs Nash on his stated understanding that she should pass on his information to the salvor; and was disturbed to discover that this had not been done.

Mrs Nash had also written to the curator of the Department of Maritime Archaeology, Western Australian Museum, Freemantle. We have no copy of her letter but may draw our own conclusions from the reply the curator, Mr Jeremy Green, wrote on June 7. "I can appreciate your problem, as I have seen similar situations occurring in Europe and the United States. Really the only solution in a situation like this is to use it as a case for legislation" he replied. "We had a similar situation occur here in Western Australia, where a Dutch East Indiaman with a lot of silver on board was discovered. The finders fell out, and there was a lot of looting. Following this the State passed legislation to protect this site and others."

Mrs Nash's concern for the *Sacramento* extended to going to Cape Town to appeal to the Historic Monuments Commission to declare the cannon a national monument – which would have resulted in David being unable to sell the gun by auction. Presumably Mrs Nash acted in the knowledge that David and Gerry had contacted Sotheby's both in Johannesburg and London with a view to valuing the cannon – and, mistakenly on Gerry's part in London, to suggest a sale.

Soon after Mrs Nash returned from Cape Town, Bird wrote in the *Evening Post* "One of the cannon recovered from the site of the *Sacramento* wreck of Port Elizabeth has been proclaimed a national monument. This means the cannon will be protected for posterity and may not be taken out of South Africa.

"A spokesman for the National Monuments Council in Cape Town confirmed this week that the proclamation had been issued.

"He said the five members of the Port Elizabeth salvage team that recovered the cannon had been informed of the proclamation. They had 30 days in which to object.

"It is understood that one of the reasons for proclaiming the cannon a national monument is that there was a danger that it might be sold overseas and so be lost to South Africa."

Astonished at the story, David and Gerry, together with their friend and legal advisor, lawyer Eric de Villiers, flew to Cape Town to request a meeting with the Monuments Commission. Immediately they sat down they sensed a hostile attitude, and at first the meeting was tense and awkward. Slowly it became clear why. The picture of the divers painted to the commission was one of a rough-necked pair of fortune hunters. Instead the Commission was confronted by a couple of young men clearly intent on obtaining the maximum archaeological benefit from their find.

The result of the meeting was that Mr de Villiers was assured by the committee that the "miracle" cannon had not been declared a national monument, only that the Commission had considered putting forward a proposal that it should be so declared at some time. In exchange the trio suggested that they would offer one of the better preserved cannon as a monument once the fate of the guns was decided. They made it clear that there was no rush to dispose of the guns.

There were however matters for the future as David and Gerry drove home that night in May well content with the day's work.

As May 20 dawned David and Gerry – with Brian MacFarlane and Peter Mason, now back from Cape Town – were eating breakfast aboard the *Gavin*, bound for the wreck site. They hoped to raise the last of the inshore cannon, which they now knew to be ship's guns. With the weather perfect and only an undulating swell, the *Gavin* with her shallow draught was able to move close inshore. It did not take Gerry long to strop and hoist six whole cannon and one half gun, the rest of which had been eroded away. David made a last check of the area and found a roll of lead carried aboard the *Sacramento* for quick repairs to the ship's hull while at sea. With six and a half guns loaded by late afternoon, the *Gavin* moved out of the surf line and David and Gerry stood in the stern looking at the site as it fell away behind the trawler heading for home for the last time.

Both men felt something of a lump in their throats in knowing that the salvage was now complete. They had found, and salvaged, a wreck of major historic importance, and had together recovered more cannon from the site than anyone else. Not bad, they felt, for their first concerted attempt at historical salvage.

In all they had brought forty cannon ashore in various states of repair. Of these twenty-one had come from the *Sacramento*'s hold; eight had been recovered from the shallows using the *Gavin*; eleven were taken from the shallows and deep vault by *Marlin*; the rest had been picked up by *Etosha*. And this had been achieved in only eleven diving days during which David had been underwater (not counting exploratory swims using only a snorkel) for forty-three hours twenty-five minutes. It was a remarkable feat simply in terms of the sheer weight of metal lifted off the sea bottom by a handful of men.

The next two events which took place were the sale of the *Gavin* by Clark in Port Elizabeth, the vessel being thought unsafe for the long voyage back to Cape Town; and the sale for scrap of some of the more badly corroded cannon, which had been certified by the museum as beyond restoration. David had wisely insisted on an agreement from the museum that the cannon should be sold.

The transaction was described by Peter Everett in the *Herald* on July 8: "Seventeen of the bronze cannon recently salvaged from the 17th century Portuguese galleon, *Sacramento*, which sank near Port Elizabeth, have been sold to metal dealers and foundries at an estimated 75 cents (South African) a kilogram . . .

Several paragraphs later Everett's story brought another angle to matters.

"Mr David Allen and Mr Gerry van Niekerk, the two Port Elizabeth divers who discovered the wreck of the *Sacramento* and the cannon, were not available for comment yesterday" the paragraph began. "A close personal friend of them both said, 'They are on Bird Island mending the jetty. I think they just wanted to get away from the back-biting.' "

Whoever the close friend was, he certainly interpreted the mood of the two men accurately.

All the cannon were moved several miles to the home of David's parents and laid out on railway sleepers on the back lawn, there to be cleaned and restored slowly as time allowed. David had approached Sotheby's of London with a request for valuation and possible auction of the cannon, but now withdrew the application saying that any sale was indefinitely postponed. Instead on New Year's day 1978 he flew to London to meet Professor Boxer and spend five weeks researching the *Sacramento* and another wreck he had found with Gerry.

Reaction to the discovery in London was markedly different from that which he had experienced in Port Elizabeth, where even old friends would not concede that he had found the *Sacramento*. In Britain enthusiasm, particularly that of academics, was unlimited after David appeared on the BBC to tell the story, and an article on the discovery appeared in the *Daily Telegraph*. Boxer greeted him as the "Only man doing anything worthwhile (in marine archaeology) on the South African coast." Mr Howard Blackmore, Keeper of Her Majesty's Firearms at the Tower of London, was thrilled by the amount of information David was able to pass on about the cannon, in particular the corroded guns had offered an insight into founding techniques never before revealed. "For once we can look into a gun and see just how it was made," Mr Blackmore said. Sir Sacheverell Sitwell wrote suggesting that David should examine the site of the battle of Lepanto which took place in the Gulf of Corinth in 1571; and Lord Kenneth Clark's grandson James, armed with an introduction from Boxer, flew from Switzerland to London to arrange to join David's team later in the year.

Explaining his London trip David said, "London is a mine of information. I'm afraid the information we were getting in South Africa was just not adequate."

By now David and Gerry had set their sights on one of the most sought after wrecks of all, the British East Indiaman *Dodington* which they knew lay on the Isles of Chaos as Perestrelo described them 400 years before – or, as it is now known, Bird Island. Find the *Dodington* they did, and the story of the salvaging, which is told in a companion volume, is one of even greater adventure than that of the *Sacramento*. While they were still working on the *Sacramento* they sailed to Bird Island aboard the trawler *Etosha* on a preliminary inspection of the island. As *Etosha* lay rolling in the heavy swell they were astonished to see a huge rainbow forming in the sky across the boat's bow, its multi-coloured end dipping into the sea in precisely the spot where they calculated the *Dodington* had lain for the past 220 years.

Appendix 1

The list below is of cannon salvaged from the site of the *Sacramento* together with the measurements of each. The question marks are inserted where there is no absolute proof that the cannon was cast by Bocarro – in most cases because the name had been worn away by the scouring action of the sand. The first cannon, here numbered 00, was found by Mr Hal Harraway in 1951, The site numbers down the left column should be read in conjunction with the site plan.

Site No.	Length (cms)	Bore (cms)	Remarks	
00	323	13	'Harraway' – C. Wegt Word C 1650	Naval
01	330	13	Bocarro C 1640	Land gun
02	308	13	?	
03	277	13	?	
04	330	13	Bocarro C 1640.	Loaded
05	285	13 (est)	?	Naval
06	296	13 (est)	?	Naval
07	336	13–13,5	?	?
08	–	13	?	Land, Loaded
09	278	13 (est)	?	?
10	288	13 (est)	?	Loaded
11	331	13,5		Land
12	281	13		Land
13	–	13		Land
14	345	13		Naval
15	286	13		Land
16	–	13		Land
17	280	13		Land
18	454	–		Land
19	433	13,5	Bocarro 1640	Land
20	324	–		Land
21	469	14	Bocarro 1640	Land
22	–	13	Bocarro 1640	Land
23	351	14	Bocarro 1640	Land
24	356	13	Bocarro 1640	Land
25	356	14	Bocarro 1640	Land
26	461	14	Bocarro 1640	Land
27	360	16,5–17	? 1637	Land
28	285	13	? ?	?
29	–	14	? ?	Land
30	–	13	? ?	?
31	461	14	Bocarro 1640	Land
32	356	14	Bocarro 1640	Land
33	360	16,5–17	1637	Land
34	461	13	Bocarro 1640	Land
35	234	12	?	Naval
36	356	14	Bocarro 1640	Land
37	356	14	Bocarro 1640	Land
38	–	13	Bocarro 1640	Land

Appendix 2

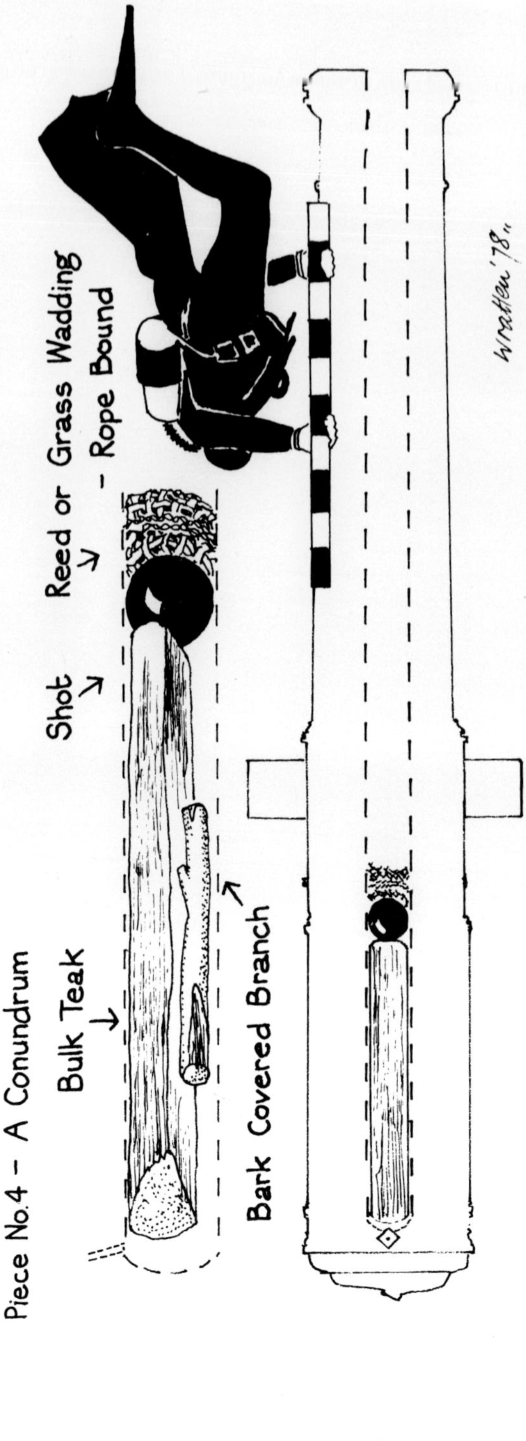

The Conundrum. This cannon was found loaded (a not unusual feature in itself because of the fear of piracy). The reed "plug" at the muzzle end of the shot might have been used to prevent the ball from running out of the barrel when the ship rolled. However the teak and piece of branch behind the shot are extraordinary. The reason for the timber and branch are still a mystery.

ROBIN GARTON
Fine Art Dealers and Publishers
9 Lancashire Court, New Bond Street, London, W1
01-493 2820

KENNETH GUICHARD: BRITISH ETCHERS 1850-1940

This fine publication, with three original etchings by Robin Tanner, has 380 illustrations and a considerable quantity of previously unpublished information.

It is the only available comprehensive survey of the British School of Etching, with biographies of some 400 artists.

Included is reference material on Muirhead Bone, Edmund Blampied, C. R. W. Nevinson and Joseph Webb.

The Folio volume is quarter bound in leather with buckram boards and gilt top edge.

ISBN 0 906030 00 5 **£50**

RAYMOND LISTER: GREAT IMAGES OF BRITISH PRINTMAKING

A survey of the magnificent achievement of British Printmaking during its heyday in the 1920's, tracing its origins to Blake and Bewick. With 64 illustrations, the book shows for the first time some of the related but varied talents which sought expression through the printed image in this country. The incomparable skill which they brought to this medium is demonstrated in its finest examples.

ISBN 0 906030 01 3 Softbound **£3.75**

HEATHER AND ROBIN TANNER: WILTSHIRE VILLAGE

An eye-witness account in word and image of a rural community, lovingly describing its ways, crafts and characters. The book holds an important place in a succession of documents such as *The Natural History of Selborne, Kilvert's Diary* and more recently *Akenfield*. Amongst these, WILTSHIRE VILLAGE is unique, for the record is illustrated by sixty meticulous drawings, faithful to their subject matter, in Robin Tanner's unmistakable style.

ISBN 0 906030 02 1 Edition limited to 100 copies, buckram and leather with Robin Tanner's etching 'The Meadow Stile'. **£75**

ISBN 0 906030 03 X Hardback **£8.95**

GEOFFREY AND DAVID ALLEN: CLIVE'S LOST TREASURE

Faced with the challenge of driving the French from India, Robert Clive booked a passage in the East Indiaman *Dodington* for his voyage out in 1755. At the last moment he switched ships but left in *Dodington* the major part of his wealth—£3,000 in gold coin. Also aboard the ship was a company of 200 soldiers and her valuable cargo included 36,000 ounces of silver in pieces of eight. In her hold were cannon, for the defence of India, sent on the orders of George II.

The ship struck Bird Island off Port Elizabeth. Only 23 men survived and they remained there for eight months while a sloop was built from the wreckage. In great physical hardship, troubled by both mutiny and piracy, the survivors sailed some 800 miles to Lourenço Marques.

Over two centuries later a team of divers headed by David Allen found the fabled wreck of the *Dodington*. Their salvage work was perilous for Clive's treasure was jealously 'guarded' by Great White Death Sharks. *Dodington* is the first British East Indiaman to have been salvaged and the find has been hailed as a major archaeological triumph.

ISBN 0 906030 07 2 Hardback **£8.95**

MARTIN MUNCASTER: THE WIND IN THE OAK
The Life, Work and Philosophy of Claude Muncaster. Foreword by H.R.H. Prince Philip.

An affectionate and vivid biography of the prolific and greatly respected painter of dramatic seascapes, pastoral landscapes and industrial scenes by his son, the well-known broadcaster. Extracts from his diaries document a varied life. He writes with equal clarity and perception of the gruelling passage in the sailing ship *Olivebank* and the calm, meticulous proceedings at Balmoral and Sandringham where he stayed. He went on to execute some of the most prestigious commissions offered in the post-war years, both by the Royal Family and famous industrialists. The scale of some of the subjects was so vast that painting from a helicopter was the only solution.

ISBN 0 906030 05 6 Hardback **£8.95**